PENG

A Life Removed

Rose George was born in 1969. After three years as senior editor at *COLORS* magazine, she became a freelance writer in 1999. She writes for the *Independent on Sunday*, the *Guardian*, the *Sunday Telegraph* and others, on subjects ranging from the alternative world cup final in Bhutan to Afghan beauty salons to Saddam Hussein's birthday. She lives in London.

PENGUIN BOOKS

# A Life Removed

*Hunting for Refuge in the Modern World*

ROSE GEORGE

PENGUIN BOOKS

To my family, for being my constant shelter.

PENGUIN BOOKS

Published by the Penguin Group
Penguin Books Ltd, 80 Strand, London WC2R 0RL, England
Penguin Group (USA) Inc., 375 Hudson Street, New York, New York 10014, USA
Penguin Books Australia Ltd, 250 Camberwell Road, Camberwell, Victoria 3124, Australia
Penguin Books Canada Ltd, 10 Alcorn Avenue, Toronto, Ontario, Canada M4V 3B2
Penguin Books India (P) Ltd, 11, Community Centre, Panchsheel Park, New Delhi – 110 017, India
Penguin Group (NZ), cnr Airborne and Rosedale Roads, Albany, Auckland 1310, New Zealand
Penguin Books (South Africa) (Pty) Ltd, 24 Sturdee Avenue, Rosebank 2196, South Africa

Penguin Books Ltd, Registered Offices: 80 Strand, London WC2R 0RL, England

www.penguin.com

Published in Penguin Books 2004

1

Copyright © Rose George, 2004

All rights reserved
The moral right of the author has been asserted

Set in Monotype Bembo
Typeset by Rowland Phototypesetting Ltd, Bury St Edmunds, Suffolk
Printed in England by Clays Ltd, St Ives plc

Except in the United States of America, this book is sold subject
to the condition that it shall not, by way of trade or otherwise, be lent,
re-sold, hired out, or otherwise circulated without the publisher's
prior consent in any form of binding or cover other than that in
which it is published and without a similar condition including this
condition being imposed on the subsequent purchaser

# Contents

Map: The Travels of Mary
Kamara and Francis Fladé
Nemlin                                    vi

1. University of Bullet                    1

2. All the Devils Have Danced            23

3. Basketball Graves                     46

4. The Rebel Business                    57

5. Woman Da Wat?                         77

6. Job Title: Refugee                    99

7. New Jersey City                      120

8. Odyssey                              153

9. It Can Happen to Anybody.
   Why Not?                             169

10. Phone Home                          175

11. Totalpeace                          206

Acknowledgements                        215

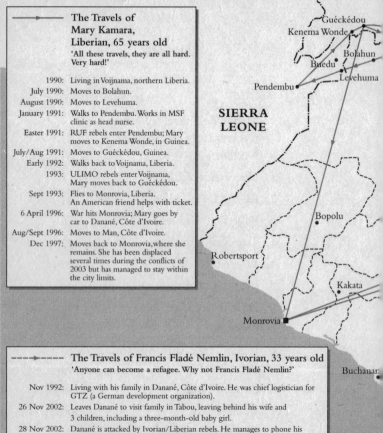

## The Travels of
## Mary Kamara,
## Liberian, 65 years old
'All these travels, they are all hard. Very hard!'

| | |
|---|---|
| 1990: | Living in Voijnama, northern Liberia. |
| July 1990: | Moves to Bolahun. |
| August 1990: | Moves to Levehuma. |
| January 1991: | Walks to Pendembu. Works in MSF clinic as head nurse. |
| Easter 1991: | RUF rebels enter Pendembu; Mary moves to Kenema Wonde, in Guinea. |
| July/Aug 1991: | Moves to Guéckédou, Guinea. |
| Early 1992: | Walks back to Voijnama, Liberia. |
| 1993: | ULIMO rebels enter Voijnama, Mary moves back to Guéckédou. |
| Sept 1993: | Flies to Monrovia, Liberia. An American friend helps with ticket. |
| 6 April 1996: | War hits Monrovia; Mary goes by car to Danané, Côte d'Ivoire. |
| Aug/Sept 1996: | Moves to Man, Côte d'Ivoire. |
| Dec 1997: | Moves back to Monrovia, where she remains. She has been displaced several times during the conflicts of 2003 but has managed to stay within the city limits. |

Guéckédou
Kenema Wonde
Bolahun
Buedu
Levehuma
Pendembu

**SIERRA LEONE**

Bopolu

Robertsport

Kakata

Monrovia

Buchanar

## The Travels of Francis Fladé Nemlin, Ivorian, 33 years old
'Anyone can become a refugee. Why not Francis Fladé Nemlin?'

| | |
|---|---|
| Nov 1992: | Living with his family in Danané, Côte d'Ivoire. He was chief logistician for GTZ (a German development organization). |
| 26 Nov 2002: | Leaves Danané to visit family in Tabou, leaving behind his wife and 3 children, including a three-month-old baby girl. |
| 28 Nov 2002: | Danané is attacked by Ivorian/Liberian rebels. He manages to phone his family and advises them to head for Liberia. Everywhere else is cut off. |
| 29 Nov 2002: | All phone lines to Danané are cut. |
| 7 Dec 2002: | Francis crosses the border into Harper, Liberia. |
| 13 Dec 2002: | Travels to Plibo by car. |
| 14 Dec 2002: | Arrives in Ganta at 2 a.m. |
| 15 Dec 2002: | Arrives in Kahnple where he finds his family in a transit centre. He now has 16 dependants (his cousin's family is there too). |
| 1 Jan 2003: | The family travels to Ganta where someone lends them a room for 2 nights. |
| 3 Jan 2003: | The family travels to Plibo and registers at the transit centre. |
| April 2003: | Francis crosses alone into Côte d'Ivoire, arriving at Tabou. He then travels to Abidjan to find work with an NGO. |
| Early May 2003: | His family flee Plibo when MODEL forces attack it, and go to Georgetown, Côte d'Ivoire. |
| June 2003: | They all meet in Tabou. |

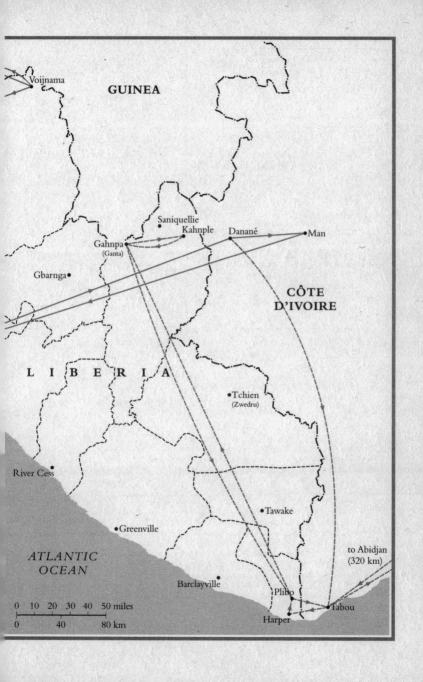

# 1. University of Bullet

'Today, Charles Taylor has liberated the Liberian people. At least, over 20,000 of them have been liberated to the great beyond.'

(Nigerian newspaper *This Day*, on Charles Taylor's arrival in Nigeria, August 2003)

A young man in Cricklewood is watching on television a country that he used to belong to. Rich is watching it from 3,175 miles and 13 years distance, because he's from Liberia, which used to be known for its exports of timber and rubber, but whose biggest export now is refugees. Three-quarters of a million Liberians are still on the run from his country, or a quarter of the population. That's equivalent to 12 million British people, or more than the population of London. Emptied.

The camera pans over Monrovia, Liberia's once-gracious capital on the Atlantic Ocean. I see buildings and waves. The young man sees memories.

'Man,' he says, in his half-London, half-Liberian accent. 'There's nothing left!'

Conversations with Liberians can be confusing. For anyone unschooled in the country's recent history, a discussion would probably go like this:

When did you leave your home?
*When the war met me.*
Which one?

Who raped your mother?
*The rebels.*
Which ones?

When did you leave Liberia?
*Which time?*

How was your child killed?
*Which one?*

It is hard to keep up with the succession of men, women and guns who have destroyed a country. Here's a short list: PRC, LPC, NPFL, INPFL, ULIMO-J, ULIMO-K, LURD, MODEL. Here are some names: Samuel, Charles, Prince, Roosevelt, George. Innocuous names, for lethal men.

I ask refugees why these men made war.

'I don't know!' they said. 'Just to destroy.' Liberia used to be a good place to be. It worked, more or less.

'Before 1989,' Liberians tell me, 'there was no such thing as a Liberian refugee.' People would go abroad to study and almost always come home. With a US dollar economy, stability and Atlantic surf, why wouldn't they?

On a bridge in Monrovia, some weeks earlier, a boy was selling sweets. They were laid out, in red wrappers, along the narrow top of a waist-high barrier. One by one, in a long and dainty line. He was selling them singly, because one sweet can be a luxury in a country only months away from battles so bad that Liberians refer to them without irony as World Wars One, Two and Three. The red sweets look like shards of glass. They are beautiful, against the damaged stone of the bridge, and behind them there are bullet holes.

Between June and July 2003, the time of the World Wars, this bridge was the stage for prancing boy and girl soldiers, in filthy clothes and crazy wigs, with heavy guns and drugged eyes, who delighted news cameramen and terrified every-one else. They were from both sides of the battle – LURD (Liberians United for Reconciliation and Democracy) rebels on one side, militia loyal to President Charles Taylor on the other. They gave themselves fine cartoon names, like Jungle Fire or University of Bullet. They were all undisciplined and dangerous, from the government soldiers launching mortars from the Monrovia side of the bridge, to the young rebels receiving them on Bushrod Island, which they now occupied. They had got far enough into the city to write 'No Monkey!' graffiti on the walls. The monkey is Charles Taylor, now ex-president of Liberia, so-called because – the versions vary – he was up in the tree and wouldn't come down, or because he was up in the tree, and he kept taking the best fruit.

Taylor's militia fighters were firing mortars from a tall build-ing overlooking the bridge, and their Small Boy Unit colleagues were down on the ground, shooting indiscriminately because that's what they did best, and that's what they'd been doing for most of the previous fourteen years, if they'd been alive that long. Occasionally, either for clearly thought-out political advantage, or because they felt like it, the fighters in the tall building would lob a rocket or two into Mamba Point, the chic quarter overlooking the ocean where the Americans had built an embassy complex that was once the largest in sub-Saharan Africa and which even today is the size of a small, highly sandbagged village. There were Liberians sheltering in the embassy compound, because they had heard there was an elec-tronic device installed there that could deflect missiles, when the rockets fell and sliced up twenty people. Later, there were Liberians lying on the ground in front of the US embassy gate number 1, because the city's residents had got too disgusted with the Americans' refusal to intervene, and piled up bodies –

killed by mortars in Greystone, the embassy's residential annex, the day before – as an incontrovertible message. In case the Americans still didn't get it, the bodies were accompanied by a handwritten note saying, 'America! What else do you want to SEE?'

The Americans didn't get it in the way the Liberians would have wished. They refused to send an American peacekeeping force, like the one the British sent to neighbouring Sierra Leone, or the French sent to Côte d'Ivoire, though an American assessment team strongly recommended intervention. Instead, several years too late, the US put its strength behind the promise of 15,000 peacekeepers. Not Americans: as usual, developing countries were to supply the majority of Blue Helmets. This helped get rid of Charles Taylor, who was persuaded to step down, and now lives in comfortable exile in Calabar, Nigeria, with a large entourage and a large phone bill. A month or so after the bodies at the gate, Liberians had a fragile kind of peace. The last time they had any peace more durable than that was in 1979.

I remember the television coverage from summer 2003, the garish boy fighters, the undertones of excitement of reporters getting to see somewhere comprehensively and newsworthily destroyed. I paid some attention, I felt some pity. But I still thought Monrovia was a country, and Freetown was its capital. Liberians in the UK say most people think they're from Libya. 'They know Sierra Leone, because it was a British colony,' says Rich's mother Grace. 'But not us. If they were in the merchant navy, they'll know us from the Liberian flags of convenience.' (Liberia has the second largest shipping fleet in the world.) When Graham Greene travelled through Liberia in 1936, he called his book *Journey Without Maps*, because there weren't any of Liberia. When I looked for a map in London's best map shop, things had progressed. There was just the one available. In German.

It is a small country – smaller than England – but even before it provided the spectacle of war, there were reasons Liberia should have stood out. On a corner in Monrovia, just before the Presidential Drive which leads past the Executive Mansion and which Charles Taylor forbade any citizen from driving down, there are three battered posters. The one with the biggest dimensions and biggest dents is the one to remember. Two cartoon figures face each other, a small man in shorts and a tall man in a stars-and-stripes hat. Behind them, there is a winding road, with way stages of Liberia's history marked out. The small figure – Liberia – has a grievance. 'We have come a long way, big brother,' his speech bubble says. 'But it's still rough. We are still suffering.' Uncle Sam looks puzzled, perhaps because he's now speaking Liberian. 'For true?' he says, meaning 'Really?'

In reality, most Americans would have no time for the small figure, because they wouldn't know he existed. But they should. Liberians call themselves America's little brother, or America's stepchild. They think they're the fifty-first state. They have a town called Harper and a county called Maryland, and there are enough children called George and Jefferson to make Republicans and Democrats proud. Monrovia is named after US President James Monroe. The Lone Star flag is a single-issue version of the Stars and Stripes: the single star represents the lone independent state in Africa in 1847, when Liberia was founded, and the eleven stripes are the eleven men who signed the Declaration of Independence. The country's motto – 'the love of liberty brought us here' – would look fine on an American licence plate. There were even stories, when the economy was good, of wealthier Liberians who lived in the US and commuted to Monrovia. 'We don't think of ourselves as an African nation,' someone says. 'We are an American nation in Africa.' African-American-Africans.

There are genuine historical roots for the belief. In 1792 Toussaint L'Ouverture began a successful slaves' revolt in Haiti. American slave-owners were alarmed enough for the repatriation of freed slaves to Africa to seem like a good idea. The American Colonization Society was formed, and volunteers were found among free slaves. In March 1820 eighty-six returnees landed at Sherbro Island in Sierra Leone, and two years later, after nearly half had been killed by malaria and disease, they came to Liberia, or the land that later took the name. They easily convinced King Peter, the local African leader, to sell them some land. He didn't have much choice, as Lt Robert Stockton was pointing a pistol at his head. The treaty, signed in 1825, ceded Cape Mesurado for 500 bars of tobacco, three barrels of rum, five umbrellas and ten pairs of shoes, among other things. Settlers kept arriving, and in 1847 the country officially began, with the octoroon Joseph Jenkins Roberts its first African-American president. It was named Liberia – from the Latin for 'freedom' – but the settlers had learned from their colonial masters that freedom has to be controlled. They had learned, too, how to be colonizers: the new Liberians dressed in clothes more suitable for Massachusetts than Monrovia, and built fine houses with porches that would be acceptable in Charleston. Liberia was founded by homesick exiles. From here, that looks like a fitting beginning.

Forty thousand African-Americans, Africans captured from slave ships and West Indians arrived over the next forty years. They settled along the coast, naming their towns Robertsport, Buchanan and Harper, and installed a top-down political system that created such disparity between indigenous and settler, the Boers would have been proud.

'This country started badly,' Blahmo Nelson tells me in his

fifth floor office in the Mansion. Nelson was Charles Taylor's Director of Cabinet, and is now the Director for the Scrupulous Implementation of the Peace Agreement. He still counts himself as Taylor's friend, though Nelson's mother starved to death in a war that Taylor was responsible for. But then, he likes to call Liberia's situation 'spontaneous combustion', when there was little that was spontaneous about it. He also likes to give lectures on good governance, and how Liberia's founders didn't have any. 'They ruled with a house-slave mentality. The house-slave was superior to the field-slave, and all the slaves were superior to the indigenous Africans. The only difference between the Liberian system and South Africa's was that Liberians are all black.' The same principles applied: a small minority ruled a majority, with heavy-handed unfairness. Liberia's sixteen tribes created another one, calling the Americo-Liberian settlers 'Congo people', because that's where some of the slaves captured from departing ships had been stolen from, though this of course offended the non-African – or less African – Americo-Liberians. They were effective rulers, both at repressing the natives and doing business. In 1927 the legislature signed a deal with US rubber company Firestone, which wanted to kick America's dependence on British rubber. It got a million acres for 99 years, at 8 cents an acre, on condition that Liberia took on a US$5 million loan. So Firestone got a deal, and Liberia got noticed. In 1943 Liberia declared war on Germany because the US asked it to. It gave its ports for the refuelling of submarines, and supplied rubber to the Allies when the Japanese took over the rubber plantations in the Far East.

By the late twentieth century, Liberia was the Dubai of West Africa. It used the US dollar for currency, and this made it a magnet. The University of Liberia (motto: *lux in tenebris* – 'light in darkness') was filled with Nigerians and South Africans. Ghanaians came to marry Liberian women. Africans from all over came to do their shopping. Monrovia was the standard stop-over. The first cheque to the African National Congress was reportedly signed by the Liberian government, and Nelson Mandela is rumoured to have had a Liberian passport.

Liberia was attractive financially and politically. In Cold War times it became strategically crucial, because the US was desperate to tame the mischief-making Colonel Qaddafi, not far north in Libya. The Americans built their huge embassy. They installed the CIA headquarters for sub-Saharan Africa here, as well as a Voice of America radio station and the Omega listening post. They made a pact with Liberians to turn the airport of Robertsfield – now Monrovia's only airport, since Charles Taylor closed the other one because it was too close to his mansion – into a US air base in twenty-four hours. This pact is still intact. When the indigenous sergeant Samuel K. Doe had President William K. Tolbert killed in 1979, and started his revolution, for a while Liberia got more aid than any other country in the region. By the time Doe was captured in 1990, and bled to death after treatment by rebels working for Prince Johnson and his INPFL (Independent National Patriotic Front of Liberia), the country was run by corrupt, venal officials. And from then on, things got worse. The country was run by corrupt, venal officials, and plundered by corrupt, venal rebels.

Liberians always call armed men 'rebels', even if the cause of their rebellion isn't usually clear. Sometimes they're not rebelling against anything. In 1995, the *New York Times* magazine ran a story about Liberia entitled, 'A war without purpose in a country without identity.' Neither assertion is true. The war in Liberia was about power and money, like most wars. It was calculated in its intent, even if the foot soldiers were anything but. 'The way we think about Liberia is strongly influenced by images of chaos and random violence,' wrote US academic William Reno in his book *Warlord Politics and African States*. In fact, 'warlord pursuit of commerce has been the critical variable in conflicts there.' Warlords are businessmen. The biggest warlord of all, future president Charles Taylor, promised to make Liberia into Hong Kong. He also promised not to be a wicked president. He didn't deliver on either count.

The world's first African republic now has the world's largest peacekeeping force for the world's worst country. Some of this is arguable; the peacekeepers are supposed to be 15,000 strong, but so far only 9,000 have been deployed. The *Economist* voted Liberia the worst place to live in the world in 2003, but that was before the peace agreement. Even so, Nicky Smith agrees with it. She's the country director of the International Rescue Committee (IRC), which is hosting my trip here. Nicky – who used to work for Médecins Sans Frontières (MSF) the aid world's shock troops, and featured as one of the year's 'heroines' in the women's monthly *Glamour* – has worked in all the guilt-spots of the world: Iraq, Kosovo, Afghanistan. She says Liberia is in the worst state of all. Because it stopped being a state, years ago.

In the words of the UN:

> Liberia is in a state of acute crisis. The majority of the population has no access to healthcare. Malnutrition is endemic. Disease is rampant. Few hospitals are operational. There is little to no public infrastructure: most schools have been shut down and clean water and functioning sewers are scarce. The economy is in a catastrophic state and tools and seeds have not arrived for the next planting season. The arrival of international peacekeepers is also behind schedule.

A quarter of the population has had to leave their homes; hundreds of thousands are dead; one in six women has been raped; at least 20,000 children were turned into soldiers; 63 per cent of the population is illiterate (87.5 per cent of rural women); only 26 per cent have access to fresh water; unemployment is at 80 per cent; half of Liberia lives on less than 50 cents a day.

These numbers should be compelling, but they probably aren't. They're probably just page-turning. It's hard to feel sorry for numbers, and refugees always travel by tide or mass.

I look at the numbers and wonder how it is that 'exiles' get prizes (I think of Edward Said, or Albert Einstein, and see awards ceremonies and intellectual glory), and 'refugees' get corn–soy blend biscuits (I think of refugees, and I see people streaming down a dusty road in Tanzania, their houses on their heads, or sitting in passive despair among tents and trauma). The dictionary thinks that an exile is exiled through a 'formal political decree', but that both 'exile' and 'refugee' undergo 'enforced voluntary absences'. It must be because an exile is always singular; refugees are always plural. An exile has a personality; a refugee is just a problem.

During my stay in West Africa, I meet a lot of personalities. I meet teachers, cleaners, drivers, politicians, soldiers. I meet an archbishop and a priest. I meet aid workers and evangelists, expats and amputees. Every single one of them has had to leave their home at some stage in the last fourteen years. Every single one knows what it's like to wake in the night to the sound of gunfire, to start walking down a road and not know where you're going. They have all been refugees.

The archbishop? Stuck for several months in Sierra Leone when rebels took over Monrovia's airport. The aid worker? He went out to look for rice one day and was press-ganged into working for rebels. He got home a year later and only then did his twin brother realize he was alive. The Swiss expat? He was kidnapped by rebels and had to walk for five days to get back. The teacher? She's built six houses in four years, because she had to, and can't remember how many houses she built before that. They've all been looted.

In the categories of humanitarian aid, some of these people are refugees, and some are IDPs (internally displaced persons). Some wear suits and ties and nice dresses. They earn salaries and for now, as Liberians say, 'things are OK.' But nothing is definite. No one is above it. A health worker, healthy and glowing in her office in Monrovia, mentions suddenly that the best way to carry your mobile phone is in your knickers. She's very precise – you don't put it in your pubic area, because the women rebels always rifle there first. You put it behind you, in your backside. I think she really means 'in', not next to. She's only being practical.

Don't be fooled by appearances in Liberia. Don't be fooled by the bustling streets of Monrovia, by the typewriting scribes tapping out résumés in the concrete loggia of the Education Ministry, by the children walking to school in clean new uniforms, by the activity and motion of this city, by the beauty of its Atlantic beaches. 'You look at Monrovia,' says Mary Kamara, a health worker, 'and you think it can't be true that all those people died!' But Monrovia is full because Liberia is empty. Pushed and shoved from one place to another, anyone who didn't end up in another country is now here, squeezed among the roofless buildings and the sandbags. There are a million people in the capital city, or 40 per cent of the population. The streets are full because the city is overflowing. The beaches are where the bodies were buried during the bad times. 'Last summer,' says Mary, 'you couldn't put your foot on Broad Street, because the bullets were flying.' This year, there is only bustle and business and hopeful enterprise: a wheelbarrow

painted with the words 'John T. Williams Transportation
Company'. A shoe-cleaner, sitting on a grimy pavement, has
painted on his metal tin that this is Uncle D's Shoe Repairing
Area. It's best to be quick about making money, when you
don't know how long the opportunity will last. There's a
monument nearby, which could stand as Liberia's motto:
erected by the Liberian government to commemorate the
Geneva Convention, it proclaims that 'even wars have limits.'
But there's a shopkeeper who has a stronger message than any
monument: his store is called Living Proof.

Monrovia, 2004, six months into peacetime. There's not
enough running water. There's hardly any electricity. On pave-
ments and dirt mounds, you see clothing laid out to dry, by
people who have neither homes nor washing lines. There is
washing, too, in every black and abandoned building, even the
roofless ones. Every inch of shelter has been grabbed, because
there are a million people needing it, and the city isn't large. It
is the equivalent of a whole town moving into one building. In
fact, a whole town did move into one building, when the
Masonic Temple – where Liberia's elite solidified their privilege
– turned into a displaced persons' camp with Grecian pillars
and a population of 11,500 people. People are still economical
with space. I see a man having his hair cut in a barber's shop
in a ruined bus shelter, the pink of the gown covering him
contrasting prettily with the blackened bricks. There are no
dogs, because the soldiers shot them and the people ate them.
There are no street lights, and international visitors are advised
not to take taxis after dark.

There are at least a dozen newspapers in circulation, with
names like the *New Broom* and the *Heritage*. They are feisty and
popular, as the Liberian press has always been. This can be
calculated by how often Charles Taylor threw journalists in

prison. A lot. (Hassan Bility, editor of the *Analyst*, became an Amnesty International prisoner of conscience in 2002.) This is a country where illiteracy is rife, and literacy is prized. It's a measure of its downfall that there are no longer any bookshops. Outside the Ministry of Education, where there are typists tapping out CVs for aspiring NGO workers, Liberia's cultural riches are reduced to a few stalls selling books. I ask for novels, but there's only *Twelfth Night* and Chinua Achebe's *Things Fall Apart*, which seems appropriate. Then I ask for textbooks, and there aren't many of those either. The ministry is barely functioning, and the school system less so. Fighters demolished schools and teachers, and recruited their pupils. There are supposed to be free government schools, but the transitional government can't provide anything for free. All schools, whether government or church-run, are fee-paying, in some way or another: the 'free' schools charge 'chair fees', 'desk fees', 'teacher fees', to cover all the things that are missing.

But there is a copy of *Our Country, Liberia*, Social Studies Book Three, last published in 1998, just after the elections won by Charles Taylor, when Liberians were fooled into thinking things were going to be all right, that maybe things wouldn't fall apart. I read in *Our Country, Liberia*, about a country that used to exist. It had a constitution, which most Liberians bring up in conversation at least once, because they're proud of it. (It was modelled on the US version, but Liberia's reportedly also forbids the wearing of flip-flops – 'slippers' in Liberian – while driving.) I read that there are gracious mansions in Liberia. Freed slaves built porches and tall rooms to copy the houses of their masters in the southern States. But they're along the coast, where it's too dangerous to travel, or if they're in Monrovia, they are burned and blackened and I don't notice them. Maybe the burned buildings along Sinkor were gracious fourteen years ago; now they house furniture shops, so you see soft plasticky couches – African kitsch – against blackened stone. They look like a guerrilla advertising gimmick. Or they look like hope.

There aren't many buildings that look relatively undamaged, and they can be categorized quite easily. Either they are necessary and governmental or necessary and financial. Of the former, the Executive Mansion has survived, despite its being looted and decaying. It is so ugly I wish it hadn't. It still serves as the seat of power, though Liberia no longer has a president, only a Chairman of the Transitional Government. The Mansion maintains the trappings of power such as security guards, plastic badges for visitors and echoing halls. But it lacks an elevator, which is disruptive to protocol: the most important people traditionally get the highest offices, because they have more ocean breeze. I only ascend to the relative obscurity of the fifth floor, but that's ten flights of stairs in 90-degree heat. (Two other reasons to knock the mansion down and start again: it was where a former president was murdered in his bed, and where a refugee in Abidjan tells me that he was held in a hole in its gardens for a month, in his own filth.) In the necessary and financial category are Western Union and DHL, both gleaming, though Western Union stopped functioning in summer 2003 because too many people were robbing their customers. There were no functioning banks by then, so Western Union – a financial umbilical cord to the world outside the wars, to the immigrants in the US and the UK sending back their salaries – was the quickest route to dollars.

The churches are well kept, too, because, as people say now, 'God is the only man we can rely on,' and they pay for his upkeep accordingly. One Lutheran church has 5,000 people on its books, and 2,000 turn up regularly every Sunday, figures which would have any English vicar in a state of religious ecstasy. In Liberia the faith business is clearly lucrative, given the good upkeep of the buildings, and everyone's getting in on it: on Somalia Drive, on the way to Robertsfield airport, before the road turns into a streak of tarmac cutting through trees, enterprising Liberians have turned their wooden swamp shacks into God huts. The Mountain of Effective Prayers, which I would report to the advertising standards authority, given the state Liberia is in, is a ramshackle hut up a dusty drive, more gin-joint than house of Jesus. I've yet to meet a Liberian atheist, though they have lived through enough to breed at least some doubt in a benevolent God.

There are celebrity houses that have survived or been rebuilt, behind big walls. The Liberian footballer George Weah – former Manchester City and AC Milan forward, FIFA World Player of the Year in 1995 and a national superhero ever since – has a white and blue mansion near the beach in Congo town. It was attacked in 1996, after Weah had said he'd like to try for president, and the raiding party was led by one of the president's trusted thugs, George Dwannah – Jack the Rebel, to his enemies – who brought seventy soldiers along for fun. They lined up the men outside and sent the women back inside, with the promise that they would be entertaining seven soldiers each. They were as good as their word: all the women were raped, including Weah's two teenage cousins. The house was looted to its limits. Later, Weah found his dining room table in the house of a Taylor ally. But now it looks protected and cared-for, and I wonder how much it costs to protect it against looters, or armed robbers, as they've become. George Weah lives in Ghana these days, so I wanted to interview him as Liberia's biggest celebrity refugee (though again, he's up against Taylor). But he came back to Liberia the week after I left, as a UNICEF goodwill ambassador. This was characteristic. Throughout the wars, he would still come home when he could easily have stayed away, and paid US$2 million of his money for the national team's plane tickets to fixtures, for their kit and upkeep.

He would hand out money at Christmas. Liberians call him King George. Charles Taylor killed people and ruined a country. If there's a competition for the nation's affections, there's no contest.

Jewel Taylor, third wife of Charles Taylor – usually described as a 'trained economist', as if no one is quite sure how an intelligent woman could end up with a man like him – has a large house by the main road through Sinkor, which looks undamaged, and has giant 'Season's Greetings' in garish lettering on the wall. Odd, in 80-degree heat, but no odder than anything else.

I'm staying in the Royal Hotel on the same road. They're building an extension, because disaster is good for business. My room has been priced for UN workers and diplomats: US$125 a night, or six times an official Liberian government worker's monthly salary, now they're getting paid again. It's Lebanese-owned, like most successful businesses here. The Lebanese own the well-stocked supermarkets, where Liberians can buy bottled Lebanese water, in a country that has plentiful rainfall. They are well connected: Charles Taylor couldn't have got a lot of his illegal shipments – he would send logs out and arms back – without his Lebanese friends. In Côte d'Ivoire, London and Sheffield, Liberians ask me what Monrovia is like these days and sooner or later they will all ask the same thing. 'Are the Lebanese still there?' Yes, I say, and there are more coming.

The Lebanese own the Royal, and they own Mamba Point Hotel, too, where the terrace restaurant charges London-level prices, and the city's visiting and resident white helpers and interventionists come for gin and tonics and the sound of the waves and the electricity generator. I have dinner there one evening with Nicky Smith, whose IRC house is just over the road, complete with security guards. (The guards are needed:

one aid worker woke up in the night to the sound of footsteps in the yard, and the shadow she saw at her window had a clearly defined AK47 on his shoulder.) A man stops us in the car park. He's sick. Nicky advises him to go to the MSF clinic down the street, but he's already been there. She tells him to go back there. He says, actually all he wants is to go home.

Last summer, Mamba Point was the press hotel, and it was a strategic location. The American embassy is round the corner, on UN Drive. Photographer Chris Hondros was in the hotel when the shells started falling. He was wondering how to cover the story, when the story came to him, in the sound of a shattering boom. Outside, a boy who'd been fetching cassava leaves was bleeding on the street. Down the road in a school, a woman had taken a direct hit. He described it in a dispatch for *The Digital Journalist.*

'"There is still the woman," someone said. "She's dead, I told you," I said.

'He seemed confused. "But look," he said simply, motioning to her through the window. And outside, the woman, who'd been directly hit by a mortar shell and nearly sheared in two, was attempting to sit up off the pavement. My head lolled down on my chest in despair.'

Later, Hondros walked back to the dark hotel, where Liberian local militiamen had watched the shell hit. 'They had no sympathy, only scorn. "You see Liberia, white man? You see how we live?"'

Liberians speak a lovely laconic English, with cadences of the American south, from where the freed slaves came in the early nineteenth century to found Africa's first republic. The worst disaster is 'not easy'. An even worse disaster is 'a bit of a problem for us'. Where our newspapers try to convey disaster with words emptied of meaning from overuse – 'plight . . . slaughter . . .

fleeing . . . human tide' – Liberians keep it simple. 'I been running for fourteen years,' they say. 'Running, running, running.' They mean it literally. They mean eight hours a day marching with swollen feet. They mean running for their lives, with gunshots close behind.

They ask, 'Can you imagine?' But it's hard. This is my second time in Africa. The first time, I went to Burundi. Like here, the capital was in the hands of the government, but the country was not. Like here, there was a veneer of normality – there, sailing on Lake Tanganyika, here the pool at the Coconut Grove compound. They called it the Bujumbura bubble. For two weeks, I felt like the war was a background noise, with the volume turned down. Here, the volume is turned up occasionally, when the newspaper headline is 'Terror! Horror! Two renegade generals make mischief in Nimba county!', or when reports filter in from the out-of-bounds interior of brutality at checkpoints, of the usual activities of war.

The war is six months behind me, but it's beyond me, too. I can't imagine running for my life. Though I sit in front of one Liberian after another, and they tell me their stories with precision and detail, I can't imagine it.

At this point, I could use helpful examples to make up the conceptual shortfall. Like saying that 50,000 refugees would fill half a football stadium. But there's no need to imagine that, because last year 50,000 displaced people did fill a football stadium, sleeping and 'toiletin' and being raped and staying hungry for months in the Samuel K. Doe stadium in Monrovia. The stadium had sixteen functional toilets.

Because this is what refugees do, mostly. There are some who pay the people-traffickers, and conform to stereotypes – bogus asylum-seeker, illegal immigrant. But most don't. They stay close to home, within decision-making distance. They just go far enough to feel slightly safer, and near enough to judge properly when they can go back.

Tabloids scream that Britain is a soft touch, but it only houses about 2 per cent of the world's 13 million refugees. In 2001 Iran and Pakistan gave refuge to 4 million people from Afghanistan. Developing countries take in 70 per cent of the world's 34.8 million displaced people, and they don't get 70 per cent of the world's gratitude. Liberia's neighbours Sierra Leone, Guinea and Côte d'Ivoire soaked up the tide of Liberians 'running, running'. There are 45,000 Liberians living in one administrative region in Côte d'Ivoire. There are 45,000 in Buduburam refugee camp in Ghana. There are some border villages with ten Liberians to every Ivorian. 'Ivorians opened their homes, shared their food,' an IRC worker says. 'I think it's pretty impressive. Would we do that?'

When Côte d'Ivoire's war broke out in September 2002, Liberia added Ivorian refugees to its visiting population, because it already had thousands of Sierra Leoneans, escaping from the unspeakably cruel tactics of Foday Sankoh and his Revolutionary United Front (RUF), which singlehandedly reduced Sierra Leone's average life expectancy to 25.9 years. When Sankoh decided he objected to elections, he developed a tactic of unassailable logic. 'No arms, no votes.' People's arms were amputated in special abattoirs, or on tree roots, or wherever was convenient. If a mother was carrying a baby on her back, troops would cut the mother's arm and then the baby's. Babies grow up into voters. Liberian refugees faced with the RUF had a choice: the arm-cutters in Sierra Leone or the looters and rapists in Liberia? Most thought the rapists were the better bet.

Africa has 12 per cent of the world's population and almost 50 per cent of the world's total of displaced people. Of the world's top-twenty refugee-producing countries, nine are African. Refugee policy analysts refer to Liberia and surrounding countries as 'a principal sub-region of displacement'. I think it's more helpful to see a pinball machine. War in Liberia – *kpow!* They hurtle into Sierra Leone. RUF in Sierra Leone – *kpow!* They hurtle back into Liberia. New rebels in Liberia – *kpow!* They are catapulted into Guinea. Conflict in Guinea – *kpow!* Back to Liberia. New rebels in Liberia – *kpow!* Côte d'Ivoire. War in Côte d'Ivoire – *kpow!* Back to Liberia. Etc., etc.

That 'etc.' isn't flippant. Mary Kamara has been running for fourteen years. 'If I started to tell you my story,' she says, 'it would never end.' She chuckles, as do her colleagues Grace and Joanne at the Women's Health and Development Programme in Monrovia, because their stories are no shorter. It is something I never get used to, the apparent inappropriateness of Liberian humour. 'I was hunted in Liberia,' a man tells me, 'so I went to Ivory Coast. I stayed there out of trouble, then the same rebels crossed the border and there they were again and the only place I could go was back to Liberia!' And his colleagues roar with laughter, because it has happened to them too. Things get so bad, they have to become funny or you will go mad. And I sit there perplexed, because I have grown up in a safe country, and I can't imagine it being different. Maybe my mother could, because she represents the last occasion most British people experienced the proper powerlessness that is part of being a refugee, in the bombs the Germans dropped, and the trains that took them as evacuees to places they didn't want to go to. Maybe I have a small idea of what it must feel like to be a refugee, from times when I have travelled alone, and felt lonely, and when that small cold feeling of panic has begun to grip my ankles. But the panic has always stopped at the knees, because I always had money, or a phone, or my belongings. In fourteen years of running, there must be a lot of places that panic can reach.

When I ask Liberians how many people need counselling, they think I'm hilarious. 'We all do!' Not just refugees or IDPs. The people in the suits in the nice cars, the children in the school uniforms, the young boys who are left on the streets after dark, who sleep on tables because they lost their family long ago, when they became child soldiers, who walk around arm in arm. 'There'll be someone just sitting here,' a counsellor tells me, 'and the next thing, they just pop and you won't understand why. People are carrying so much. Every single person walking the streets of Liberia needs counselling.' But there were only twenty-eight doctors in Liberia at the last count, and no psychiatrists. Archbishop of Monrovia Michael Francis, one of those frank-speaking priests who redeem the Catholic Church, says that 'Liberia is on its back. On its knees.'

However you want to describe it. Liberia is in meltdown.

In the living room in Cricklewood, Rich's mother Grace is watching the video too. It was filmed when Taylor was in power, so the narrator, a Liberian expat called Nancee Oku-Bright, has to be careful not to be too critical. When the Sierra Leonean film-maker Sorious Samura went to Liberia in 2000, he got permission from the Ministry of Information for a documentary about Taylor. He was still arrested, beaten and told he would be 'raped until you bleed'. So Oku-Bright doesn't comment on Taylor's chilling promise not to be a wicked president, though he'd already broken it. Grace does it for her, with a disgusted 'huh!' How could he say that? she asks. Why not? His campaign slogan was 'He killed my ma, he killed my pa, I'll vote for him.'

I found it hard to believe this, when I first heard it in Monrovia. But everyone said it was true, and it's there on the screen in Grace's living room. Laughing young women shouting it out in election rallies. Young children holding posters where it's written in big letters. I am shocked at its cruelty, and tempted to dismiss it as barbarity. Actually, Liberians were just being practical. People voted for the man who had killed their parents, because they didn't want anyone to kill the rest of the family. They voted out of exhaustion and hope. Charles Taylor was the best chance for peace Liberia had, and he won the election fairly. It's probably the only fair thing he ever did.

## 2. All the Devils Have Danced

*Liberian joke:*
How do you recognize a Liberian?
Because if you ask them where they're going,
they always say 'somewhere'.

I meet a girl by the side of the road. We'd only stopped to say hello to her foster-mother, but there's always a story to be told. Patricia is fifteen, and she has no family left. She says she was at home when they heard the sound of heavy guns. They all ran, in all directions. She says, in a standard Liberian phrase, 'We scattered. Helter-skelter.' Her mother went one way, her father another, and she hasn't seen them since. I look at her – didn't you at least try to stay together? She looks right back at me. Don't I know anything? When you hear gunfire, you run. Getting away from the sound is the only thing that matters. You are reduced to pure reaction, and there is nobody but you. When a Liberian says, 'I lost my father,' it is literal.

Cerue Gonah Karto took her baby and ran from Monrovia on 28 July 1990. Charles Taylor's rebels were approaching, and she didn't want to get caught in the crossfire. She'd never left her home before, not in this fashion. I ask her how she remembers the date, just as I ask all the refugees I meet how they remember the date, because the only dates I remember are a few birthdays and Christmas. But they know dates exactly, even from fourteen years ago. It's striking. 'Of course I remember it. You have to! It was painful. Horrible. Terrifying. You don't know where you're going, who you're meeting on the way. You've heard about rebels, you saw them on television, and you don't know who they will be, their reaction to you.'

So she tried to travel in a group, thinking it might be safer. One of the men walking with her was called Banana, 'because he played for the army football team, and he was very good. Slippery with the ball, like a banana.' Banana had kindly offered to carry Cerue's baby bag, because she was already carrying the baby tied to her back with a *lappa* (a piece of cloth used as a skirt or wrap), African-style, and travelling by foot through the bush, refugee-style. They walked for three weeks, during the daytime, 'so if you have to run, you can see where you're running to'. They came across some rebels, who recognized Banana.

'Whoah, Banana, you a Doe soldier! Why d'you come this way?'

'I'm not a soldier,' he said, 'I'm a footballer. I just played for their team.' He was carrying the baby bag, and he subtly gave it back to Cerue.

'Naah, you're here on reconnaissance,' they said, and they shot him. Seven times; Cerue counted. She would have been shot too, if a kindly rebel hadn't told her to distance herself from Banana, to hide the baby bag. 'They'll think you're the wife or sister of a soldier and kill you too.'

After that, Cerue was speechless. It's hard to imagine this now, in this confident feminist activist who refuses to grant interviews to male journalists, because 'they can wait till Liberian men wake up!' In the bush, though, education is irrelevant. Feistiness is irrelevant. All you need is luck. 'I didn't eat for one week. I was crying, I was dehydrated.' She almost killed her baby the same day, when he was crying and she put hot food in his bottle. 'I almost put it to his mouth and one of the soldiers came and said, "Sister, the food is hot. I saw steam coming out. You want to put that in your baby's mouth?"' She smiles now. 'I think I was not myself.'

I hadn't come to talk to Cerue about her story. I didn't think she'd have one. We were supposed to talk about WIPNET, the Women in Peacebuilding Network that she works for. WIPNET organizes sit-ins in the field opposite the fish market, and they carried on all through the war, even when Taylor threatened them, and even when the shelling started. 'It was very desperate and fearful, so we stopped for a couple of days. But when it quietened down, we came back.' We talked about activism, peace agreements and the stuff that WIPNET women usually talk about, in the two hundred interviews that they've given since the peace agreement.

But digression is inevitable, as Cerue says. 'I don't think any Liberian who stayed behind doesn't have a story. Either you stay in your house and you starve, or you've got something to tell.'

At Mother Patern technical college, I'd come to talk about the college's Women's Health and Development Programme (WHDP). Mary Kamara, Grace and Joanne run the programme, and they are funny, educated and articulate. They have deep, contagious laughs, and they're Liberian, so they laugh a lot. In another situation, they would be called privileged. Maybe they're privileged even here, because they're not dead. They tell me about their programme, which involves writing fiction composed of women's experiences, so that women aren't shy of talking about their own. They know what they're talking about, because they have lived it too.

What is the worst thing about being a refugee? Mary thinks about this. She is an elegant, sixty-five-year-old grandmother, on the run since 1989. She has a lot of experience to consult, before she can answer the question. Eventually, she makes that expressive African high-pitched *ha!* sound, and claps her hands together for emphasis, as Liberians do. 'When war is going on,' Mary says, 'it's confusing. You feel hopeless, helpless. You don't know what to do. Once you don't hear the guns any more, you manage other things as they come. Food, shelter, clothing, you manage. But when the war is going on, that's the worst experience you can ever go through, because you are reduced to nothing.' She taps the table for emphasis. Nut–tin. Tap tap.

The worst thing about being a refugee, Mary continues, is not knowing where you are going. War can push you anywhere, as it likes, and it can meet you round every corner. Liberians always say, 'When the war met me . . .' and I find this quaint, like the war has been personalized. But is there anything more personal? 'Being a refugee changes you completely,' a young orphaned man tells me in a refugee transit centre in Abidjan, Côte d'Ivoire. 'Being a refugee means that you are not the same as before when you were in your country. You are not the way you used to look. You don't have the freedom you had, the education, the number of family members, none of them will be the same as before. These things that change are the things that make you more worried, make you more a refugee.'

We should know this by now. The twentieth century provided enough images of families trudging down a road in wartime, their belongings in a handcart, going who knows where. But the human mind is adaptable; this is our biggest advantage and our biggest weakness.

In Abidjan, IRC employees' security briefing includes the tale of the frog in the pot. A frog sits in a pot of water, and if the water is heated slowly enough, it never jumps out. It adapts, and then it is boiled to death. Julien, the IRC's country director, told me this story because the night before, driving around Abidjan, I'd seen the shadow of a gun in a pickup full of men. I said, 'Is that a gun?' with some alarm, though it shouldn't have been a surprising sight, since Côte d'Ivoire is officially still at war; 60 per cent of the country is in the hands of rebels and, according to Foreign Office travel advisories, most of the country is too dangerous to travel to. Julien had brushed off my question as that of a naive visitor, but he brought it up again, along with the frog. When you become used to guns, you pay them less mind. When you see images of refugees fleeing, you switch them off.

In Liberia you are tuned to the sound of gunfire. On one Liberian's website, the first answer to 'How do you know if you're a postwar Liberian?' is, 'If you consider gunshots to be the sound of music.' (You are a pre-war Liberian if you 'still give directions by landmarks such as the big plum tree'. If you are still fool enough to believe in landmarks.)

Mary jumps when a door bangs. Sometimes the sound of children playing scares her. It doesn't sound like a rocket or anything, it's just – when they scream, you wonder. 'When the guns are sounding, you are living in an atmosphere of terror. I can't concentrate, I can't eat, I can't sleep. But when the guns are silent, your inside can just be hanging. You are neither with the dead or the living, you are just in between. So when the guns are silent, you are able to eat, able to lie down and sleep, and move around small. You can have some peace of mind.'

Mary is from Lofa county, one of Liberia's most beautiful. I don't go there, because the UN peacekeepers hadn't deployed there yet. But I hear there's nothing there, because people from Lofa hear that there's nothing there, that their houses are now bush. There are no schools, no buildings, a decimated people. 'I don't belong in Monrovia,' Mary says, in her gentle accent. 'But I've been here quite a while now. I've been a refugee in Sierra Leone, Guinea and Ivory Coast.' That just leaves Ghana, I say, and she laughs. 'No, I didn't get to Ghana.' She left Lofa in 1990 and walked to Sierra Leone. But then the RUF followed her, and she was chased out of Sierra Leone and into Guinea.

She went back to Liberia in 1991, but the rebel faction ULIMO arrived, and she went back to Guinea. In 1993 she took a plane to Monrovia, and stayed there for a few months. 'In 1996 war broke out and we went to Ivory Coast. When that subsided, we came back again at the end of 1997.'

She says 'subsided' not 'finished'. Liberians say 'when war subsides', as if it's a tide. Tides go back and forth, but they always come back. (See the map of Mary's journey on pages vi–vii.) They talk about 'LURD time' and 'LPC time', like we talk about ice ages or monarchs. Life is subservient to war and rebels. 'Being raped, being stripped,' says Mary. 'It's part of the game. If you survive, you're lucky, that's all.'

Grace is lucky. Grace, Mary and Joanne are sitting round a table in a noisy office at Mother Patern college. Noisy is good in Monrovia, because it means things are working. The college is up and running fine, though the University of Liberia isn't. The college's tenacity is undoubtedly partly due to the determination of the dean Sister Barbara – another of those fearless Catholics famous all over Monrovia – who stayed behind through all the wars to watch over it. The WHDP office is a small partitioned area, papered with gender-based violence posters – don't beat your woman, don't suffer her. My favourite is one showing a woman carrying two children – one by the hand, one on her back – and a weight of logs on her head, while her husband plays checkers under a tree. Grace grins at that – 'so true!' She knows about unresponsive husbands. One night last year, she was lying in bed. She lives behind the Wilson Corner displaced camp, which her friends think is brave, because the rebels attack camps quite often: a static population with some belongings to loot and nowhere to go – why wouldn't they? So she was lying there, next to her husband, when she heard noises in the yard. She kept nudging her husband, and he kept refusing to get up, like a scene from a

Liberian *Men Behaving Badly*. 'So I got up, and I put my jeans on. I was half-dressed already, because in those days you slept mostly dressed, so you could leave quickly if you had to. I put my money inside my jeans, at the front, and then there was a boom! And a soldier said, "If you don't open the door, we will shoot!"' Grace was terrified, for all the normal reasons, and because eight of the twenty-five people staying in the house were young girls. 'That time we were on the Charles Taylor front line. Soldiers were going from house to house, street to street, taking everything, raping the girls. I knew if they saw them, they would rape them. But I think there was a miracle – someone shot into the yard from the other side of the swamp. The bullet fell through the roof, and the soldiers ran away to deal with it. The next day, I packed our bags, put them on my head, and said, "We're going straight to the displaced camp. You either decide to stay and wait for the next round of soldiers to come or you pack your bag."'

Mary shakes her head. It's all too familiar. 'When that happens to you, you just don't care where you're going to lie down. You are so scared. But that's the thing that can really help us to keep moving, because at one point you are down, and the next point you are up and moving around. If there is war, we panic, we are confused. But when it subsides, we calm ourselves down and we keep moving.'

And everyone keeps moving, even if it's just to friends' houses, up and down the city. I ask Mary how she can still believe in a God who – in my agnostic opinion – doesn't seem to have been paying attention to Liberia. 'I don't think God neglected us, because we would always find someone to take us in.' Sometimes you just go and sit on a stranger's porch, and they will let you in. You don't have to knock.

But there aren't enough houses in Monrovia to shelter a whole country. 'You would see people walking on the streets, with babies on their back, and you would stand up and cry in your heart. It was the rainy season, it was pouring, but you don't even know you're wet, you're so sorry for them.'

'Like in the swamp,' Grace picks up. 'The number of children there are in that swamp . . . Their parents were running, and the children fall down, and they just drown.' She makes an African *tsk* sound, because the thought still pains her, and the children haven't yet been dead a year. 'You can't go on the road for the gunshot, so you have to go through the swamp.' But Liberians aren't great swimmers, and the swamp is deeper than the height of children. So the children still lie there, along with unknown numbers of people killed by Liberia's greedy men. Liberia's swamps must be the most fertile in West Africa.

I ask Mary how many family members she lost. There's some confusion, given what 'lost' can mean here. Grace shoots my euphemism to bits. 'She means, how many people die from you?' Mary says, 'Oh!' and starts to count. 'My mother. My father. My son. My aunt. My nephew. Maybe three aunts. Actually, I won't know until there is complete disarmament. I won't know how many are alive and how many are dead.' Grace's oldest brother was killed by ULIMO fighters. He was beheaded. They identified his skeleton later because his glasses were lying by the body. Maybe glasses weren't getting a good price at the time.

Where Grace lives, there are many ex-combatants. 'They come and ask me to draw water. I say no. I say, "You came and looted my house, you took everything from me and I will not encourage you to come back." I got no sympathy for them! If you treat them well, they will still come back after. They will still loot you.' The ex-combatants are untouchable. 'They do a crime and nobody can prosecute them. They say anything and they are not afraid to say what they have done. They are not disarmed, they have just put their arms away.'

Grace, Mary and Joanne are good Christians. But they're not ready to forgive yet. I ask Mary how many people would need to apologize to her, and she can't answer. 'I can't remember how many. We have a saying, that all the devils have danced in Liberia.' And she's not sure whether the performance has finished, or whether this is just the interval.

There are grounds for uncertainty, when the biggest devil is sitting in exile in Nigeria. It would be funny, if it wasn't so sad. The man who helped give Liberia the biggest proportion of refugees in the world is a refugee.

> BBC INTERVIEWER: They say you worked directly with the [Sierra Leonean rebel] leadership. You gave them guidance, you gave them direction, you gave them financial support, military training, personnel, arms, ammunition and other support and encouragement.
> CHARLES TAYLOR: Can't you indict a house rat? You can indict a house rat.

Charles Taylor has a US$2 million bounty on his head. He has been indicted by the Sierra Leone war crimes tribunal, which accuses him of 'greater responsibility' in causing Sierra Leone's conflicts. It should be enough to keep him out of trouble. But he's escaped jail before. He's been in exile before. Of all the dancing devils, he has the most nimble footwork.

On 11 August 2003, Cerue Gonah Karto was on the phone with a friend in America. 'He's at the airport!' said her friend. 'His left foot is on the first step! He's climbing the steps! They've shut him in the plane! The plane has taken off!' Cerue tells me this tale with all these exclamation marks, probably because she still finds it incredible. By August, the president of Liberia, thanks to considerable pressure from George W. Bush, was persuaded that exile in Nigeria was his best option. Even so, no one thought he would leave. Cerue had no television – not enough money, not enough electricity – so the phone calls from America, Europe and elsewhere were the only way Liberians could keep track. So she didn't hear until later what Charles Taylor said in his final speech before stepping down, as the presidents of South Africa, Mozambique and Ghana looked on: 'I am the sacrificial lamb. I am the whipping boy.' History would be kind to him, he said. He had done great deeds, and had served his country well. It's lucky most Liberians didn't have televisions, or the whole country would have been lifted up and down, like the shifting of tectonic plates, because so many people would have shouted *ha!* in disbelief.

Taylor finished with typical arrogance. 'God willing, I will be back.'

'That was such a cruel thing to say,' an aid worker tells me. 'So cruel.'

But not as cruel as coups can be in Liberia. When Samuel Doe overthrew William Tolbert, he had him disembowelled. When Prince Yormie Johnson killed Samuel Doe ten years later, he had Doe's ears and penis cut off and took his dismembered body on a stroll around the streets. By comparison. Taylor's leave-taking was quiet, ordered, and very out of character. Once, Taylor was interviewed by BBC *Focus on Africa* editor Robin White, as famous in West Africa as Mark Tully is in India ('Do you know him?' ask Liberians. 'Why not?'). White asked Taylor what he thought of being branded a murderer by the UN. 'Well,' he responds, with sinister charm. 'They called Jesus Christ a murderer too.'

In aid circles, Liberia is classed a Complex Emergency. But it's actually about the simple things: power, self-preservation, cynicism. It's described as ethnic conflict, because Liberia has sixteen ethnicities – seventeen, if you count the Americo-

Liberians – and there has been plenty of conflict. But like most ethnic conflicts, if you bother to look, you can see the strings. In Liberia's 'tribal warfare', cynical men pulled the strings. Someone tells me a parable about cows, as told by the Liberian intellectual Dr H. Fahnbulleh. There were three cows. One black, one white, one brown. They had one common enemy. The enemy went to the black cow and said, 'Why are your friends grazing on the other side? It's because you're black!' So the cow left his friends and was devoured by the enemy. The same happened with the white cow, and then the brown cow. 'You see,' Fahnbulleh said. 'You have to be careful. There will be lies and rumours. They will do all they can to bring disunity among you.'

And the best cow manipulator of all was Charles Ghankay Taylor. President, warlord, unholy terror.

His fighters called him Pappy, meaning 'daddy'. James T. Krah, writing in the Liberian exiles' magazine *The Perspective* on 4 February 2002, calls him other things, too: 'pariah, criminal, Bin Laden terrorist connection, jail escapee, mafia, dictator, sadist child abuser, megalomaniac, irrational, con artist, drug pusher, warlord, despot, tyrant, philanderer, impostor, buffoon, gangster.'

'I call him CT on the record,' says an Irish priest in Liberia. 'Off the record, the names I have for him wouldn't be publishable.'

Charles Taylor might not be the worst thing to happen to Liberia, but he is the most successful worst thing. There have been warlords aplenty, with varying degrees of political and economic brilliance, and much thuggery. There has been Samuel K. Doe, who voted himself president in 1985 in a clearly fraudulent election. (Doe said 51 per cent of Liberians had voted for him, but he was lying. The Americans said the election was 'not bad, by African standards'.) There have been priests who turned warlords, and teachers and aid workers. The head of the MODEL (Movement for Democracy in Liberia) faction used to work for UNICEF. They have had varying degrees of power and influence. The factional leaders of MODEL and LURD now sit in the transitional government, because the international community put them there with the Accra peace agreement of 18 August 2003.

But only Charles Ghankay Taylor, warlord, became president, in elections that must have been free and fair, because Jimmy Carter said so. Only Charles Ghankay Taylor became the first ever sitting president to be indicted for war crimes. Only Charles Ghankay Taylor, international meddler, stands accused of fomenting trouble and warfare in all three neighbouring countries. Only Charles Ghankay Taylor – with his Taylorforces, and the territory he held becoming known as Taylorland – became an adjective.

President Samuel K. Doe was an obscure army sergeant with big glasses and an army cap set at a jaunty angle, and not much of a way with words. He or his soldiers started their coup in 1979 by killing President William K. Tolbert. They followed this by shooting thirteen members of Tolbert's cabinet. There is video footage of the shooting: thirteen telegraph poles, of differing sizes, are stuck in the sand on one of Monrovia's beaches. The men – most of them elderly, most of them dignified, all stripped to their uniformly white underwear – are tied round the waist to the poles. Some of them slump around the rope. One bearded man stands upright, watching and waiting. It is a terrible scene. The soldiers fire and it doesn't look particularly accurate, so they fire again, and again. Then I'm not sure which is worse – the bodies scrunched together in a mass grave, or Liberian civilians jubilant on the beach. Laughing, shouting. There was genuine joy because Tolbert had been corrupt and inept, and his government elitist. Doe was an accidental revolutionary: there are reports he only went to the Mansion to ask for wages, and was propelled into power by being the oldest man there. His capacity for foresight was obvious with the Liberian Beach Party, as the executions became known. Because although Doe stayed in power for ten years, they were the beginning of his downfall.

One of the men he had shot was A. B. Tolbert, son of the president. Alphonse was married to Daisy Delafosse, the beloved adopted daughter of Felix Houphouët-Boigny, president of neighbouring Côte d'Ivoire, and not a man to cross. Later, she reportedly married Blaise Compaoré (I've never figured out why it's still 'reportedly'), who became the not-very-democratic president of Burkina Faso, and not a man to cross either. With one execution, Doe had alienated two countries that it would have paid to keep happy. Irritated allies can provide good shelter for rebels plotting trouble. It was stupid.

'Ach, he wasn't an educated man,' says Grace Quoi, the Liberian refugee who is watching a video of Samuel Doe with me in her north London living room. 'Look at him! Bugs Bunny!' The film shows Doe sitting next to his mother shortly after the coup, answering questions from the press. They ask about the state of the economy. 'No problem.' They ask him about the cabinet. 'No problem.' They ask him about what will happen with Liberia's US policy. 'We'll continue the same policy,' he says with a dumb grin, and he clearly has no idea what the policy is. He learned fast though, well enough to keep the US onside, despite his reign's bloody beginnings, and well enough to get US$500 million in US aid over the first five years. This made Liberia the biggest recipient of US aid in Africa, thanks to Doe's willingness to follow big brother's orders by kicking out the Libyan and Soviet diplomats and keeping Liberia firmly on the warmer side of the Cold War.

Doe was uneducated, but smart enough to see the value of an education: he and his cronies graduated from the University of Liberia while they were running the country. 'With A grades?' I ask Grace. 'Ha! Probably.' Military juntas don't get Bs. By the time Doe visited the US in 1985 – where Ronald Reagan presented him as Chairman Moe, and where he stood by Reagan's side looking dumb and foolish, and a lot less lethal than he was – he was a more educated, supposedly elected president. But he only had five years left, partly because French-speaking West Africa had not yet forgiven the beach executions, and were willing to hatch trouble for Doe. Partly, also, because he was a Krahn man, and he learned to trust nobody who was not.

The Krahn are a small tribe in Liberia. They number about 5 per cent of the population, about the same as the Americo-Liberians. The Krahn were mostly jungle people, illiterate peasants from the interior. But once Doe had started his killings, his Krahn kinsmen were his best line of defence. They were sent to Monrovia and recruited into the government and armed forces. Some of them had never seen running water before they were invited to help run a country. For the next ten years, Liberians watched their economy deteriorate in the hands of peasants. They were indigenous peasants, so they operated on revolutionary credentials, but they still destroyed an economy. By the time Charles Taylor decided to turn liberator – 'All these liberators!' says Mary Kamara. 'Who asked them to liberate us?' – there was enough resentment, poverty and frustration to fuel a rebellion.

Charles Taylor was probably everything James T. Krah paints him – I hear enough stories from Monrovia expats about weekend coke parties, and young girls buried in swamps after they have served their purpose, to believe a few of them. One expat businessman told the tale of a young man who worked in his office. 'Taylor's forces came and arrested him for treason. They locked him up for months. Then one evening, they put him in a car with a young girl, about fourteen years old, and drove up to the airfield. The car stopped, the girl was taken out and stripped, and buried alive in a hole. Another night, he was taken out again in the car, with two other prisoners, one sitting on each side of him. The car stopped, the two other prisoners were told to get out and *bam! bam!* Their heads were blown off. I can't ask him too much about it, because he's still a gibbering wreck.'

But even Liberians who have spent years hating Taylor call him 'street-smart'. He is Hollywood film material, in that brutish colourful way that Milosevic is. He is equally fascinating. 'If Charles Taylor tells you it's daylight,' a woman tells me, 'you'd better look at your watch. If he says it's black, you know it's red.' If Charles Taylor had stayed on the right side of goodness, he would have been Liberia's salvation.

He was born in 1948 in Monrovia, to an Americo-Liberian father and an indigenous Gola mother. That made him an Americo-Liberian, which was useful for as long as Americo-Liberians ran the country, which they did until 1979. His father sent him to the United States for his education, and he has an economics degree from Bentley College in Massachusetts. That's just education, though. His street-smartness was demonstrated by his ability to get a job in Doe's administration, when the most notable characteristic of Doe was that he was indigenous. Doe's coup was supposed to have eliminated the Americo-Liberian elite. The downtrodden kicked out the privileged, or such was the PR. In reality, Doe needed the elite to run the country, and he kept some on. Taylor belonged to the privileged, but by the early 1980s he was at the head of the Government Services Agency. (He got the job, the rumours go, by marching into the office when the GSA head was out, and saying he was in charge.) The agency controlled Liberia's budget, and was a honey pot, just as all state enterprises in poor countries are honey pots, and Taylor took full advantage.

By 1984 he had fled to the US, where he was arrested for embezzling $922,382 from the GSA. He was jailed at the Plymouth County House of Correction to await extradition, but he escaped. How he did it is still a matter of Liberian dinner conversation. Ask a Liberian, and they will reply. 'But you should know better than we do!' Liberians suspect the US government had something to do with it. 'If you leave money in a drawer in your bedroom,' a Liberian refugee tells me in an Ivorian village, 'and the only people who have access to it are your brother and sister, and the money is taken, who do you blame?' I say, 'The brother and sister.' He says, 'Exactly!' Case closed. Taylor has said he bribed prison guards with US$30,000 and sawed through the bars in the laundry room. Whatever happened, the next sighting of Taylor was in Libya. In a charity office in south London, where I am interviewing the head of a Liberian association, a colleague sticks his head round the door. 'I met Charles Taylor! I was in Tripoli, delivering a paper on something. I came down to the library one morning and he was sitting there reading it, in his pyjamas and dressing gown. He was very courteous.'

The next time Taylor appeared in Liberia, though, he was in full battledress. It was Christmas Eve, 1989, and his invasion was unexpected. With Ivorian and Guinean support, his NPFL (National Patriotic Front of Liberia) fighters – all 150 of them – entered Nimba county. It was easy to gather support in Nimba, because Doe's ethnic Krahn troops didn't like the Gio and Mano peoples who lived here, and massacred them regularly. Taylor's new African identity – he added Ghankay (Gola for 'strong' or 'stubborn') to his name, for extra African cred – helped gather support. For the next seven years, more or less, he led a civil war that was uncivil beyond belief. Beheadings, rape, massacres. Some fighters from NPFL split and became INPFL, led by Prince Yormie Johnson, later to kill Samuel Doe, and even later to turn into an evangelist priest in Nigeria. Some disgruntled Liberian refugees in Sierra Leone – Krahn and Mandingos, who had fled after Doe's death – formed ULIMO, which later split into ULIMO-K and ULIMO-J. Some other disgruntled Liberians formed the Liberia Peace Council, or LPC, led by George Boley, a physical education teacher who liked to call himself Doctor. The global-security.org website, run by security experts not easily defeated by complexity, characterized the civil war as 'so frighteningly gruesome that for many, it was almost impossible to understand'. All the devils danced in Liberia, and they had heavy, heavy shoes.

By mid-1990 Taylor was preparing to take Monrovia. His fighters set up checkpoints, usually a piece of rope with human skulls dangling from it for effect. Some checkpoints became so notorious, they had nicknames. A US State Department document reported one checkpoint called No Return, where 2,000 people were killed in 1990 and their bodies left to rot in the bush. I see a chilling photo of one checkpoint, where a young girl is being led away by soldiers. She is wearing only a T-shirt and knickers, and her mouth is open. Behind her, there's a long line of people waiting their turn.

Taylor didn't take Monrovia, but he did have 90 per cent of the country, which he named Greater Liberia, and which provided about US$75 million a year in diamond, rubber and timber profits. The interim government – formed in talks in the Gambia in October 1990 – had $3 billion in debts. Taylor weighed up profit and loss, and ignored the peace agreement. The rebel business was better business.

A massive NPFL assault on Monrovia in 1992 was called

Octopus, because it came on many fronts. But he may as well have used that name for the whole country, because his tentacles were everywhere. Fighters ruled the land and the sea. They just didn't have planes yet. In 1990 a Liberian businessman gave testimony to Human Rights Watch investigators. 'Even while the ceasefire was in force, fighters would go to the beach when the Kru fishermen came in. They would say that every fish in the ocean belonged to the CIC [Taylor, the Commander-in-Chief]. They would say that if you catch three fish, one is for the government, two are for you; if you catch two fish, one is for the government; if you catch one, it's for the government.'

Charles Taylor liked a joke, so he planned Octopus, his most vicious assault, even while he was supposed to be in peace talks. (He also probably arranged for the vile Foday Sankoh to march into Sierra Leone and start the RUF at the same time.) Liberians still shake their head at how appalling Octopus was, and they still know the exact date it happened. Young fighters were sent through the swamps into the city. Some lost their legs from swamp crocodiles, some drowned. There was violence, looting and terror, until the international community was stirred enough to back the presence of peacekeepers from ECOMOG (Economic Community of West African States' Monitoring Group). They pushed Taylor's forces out of Monrovia, and spent the next years trying to flush him out of ports and towns with helicopter gunships and badly aimed rockets. 'We were living in a hostel,' an IRC staff member called Vera tells me. 'My aunt, grandmother, children – every one of them died because ECOMOG had fired some rockets.' She nods, thinks about it, then says without rancour, 'I suppose they made some mistakes.'

Nothing was safe. Even the keepers of the peace brought war. Even the money you carried could get you killed. 'Money! Ha!' says Alfred Nagbe, now a refugee living in Sheffield. 'It was very complicated!' The US dollar had been abandoned in the 1980s, when Samuel Doe printed his seven-sided coins known as Doe dollars. But they were too heavy, so the JJ was introduced; a dollar substitute that had a picture of Liberia's first president, Joseph Jenkins, on the bill. But Taylor had looted so much from the bank, the interim president at the time – a respected professor named Amos Sawyer – decided to start afresh. The new money was called 'Liberty', because it featured Liberia's breathtakingly elitist national motto, 'The love of liberty brought us here' – thus excluding 95 per cent of the population. A money named freedom, in a country called freedom that had none. Yet Taylor didn't like it. Carrying Liberty into Taylorland could get you killed. Changing JJs for Liberty could also get you killed. The only functioning banks by then were in Monrovia, and it was rainy season and the roads were terrible. (To get to Monrovia from Sinoe, which seems a direct route on the map, you had to travel north to Gbarnga and down again.) People took canoes along the Atlantic instead, because the government had only given a month for people to exchange their money, but the sea was rough, and many drowned. You don't have to do anything special in Liberia to get killed. You certainly don't need to make an effort. It's as easy as a trip to the bank.

By 1992 Liberia was stifling on the inside and outside. A transitional government ruled in Monrovia, but Charles Taylor ruled in reality. The airport was closed. International flights were stopped. ECOMOG secured Monrovia, so a million people went there for safety. And rebel factions continued to multiply, just to confuse things further. By 1994 there were seven factions fighting, or seven who'd bothered to give themselves names. The INPFL had broken off from the NPFL. Alhaji Kromah, formerly the head of the Liberian Broadcasting Corporation, formed ULIMO (the United Liberation

Movement for Democracy in Liberia), which later splintered into ULIMO-K (led by Kromah), and ULIMO-J (led by Roosevelt Johnson). The dynamics were those of playground squabbles, but the spoils were huge: diamonds, rubber, timber. They were there for the taking, then the losing, then the retaking.

The Ivorian writer Ahmadou Kourouma describes this better than most in his novel *Allah n'est pas obligé*. Published in 2000, it describes the trials and travels of child soldier Birahima, as he wanders through the sub-regional war zones of Côte d'Ivoire, Liberia and Sierra Leone. The title comes from his conviction – being a good Muslim boy – that 'Allah isn't required to be fair in all the things he's created down here.' If not, he could be held accountable for such unfairness as the vile business methods of INPFL leader Prince Yormie Johnson, described masterfully by Kourouma in fiction that is truthful.

Prince Johnson wants to control 'the largest American rubber company'. He proposes himself as its security chief, offering to deal with the bandits who are bothering the Americans. 'The president explains patiently that if he gave him the job of securing the rubber plantation, that meant he recognized him as the sole authority in Liberia. He couldn't do that, because the other factions wouldn't let him.' Johnson didn't seem convinced. He went back to his camp and reflected. Three days later, three workers disappear. Johnson returns them in their underpants, saying he'd found them. The president offers him a reward. Johnson refuses. The president doesn't get it. A month later, three workers and three black officials disappear. They are returned naked. 'Johnson gave them back to the president with compassion, because they were incomplete. The three workers had had their right hands amputated, and the black officials their two ears.' The president still didn't get it. Six weeks later, four workers, three black officials and one white American disappear. When the black officials were returned, they were missing their ears and right hands. One of them was more incomplete, consisting only of a head. 'And Johnson explained with a smile that the bandits were still holding the four blacks and the white man. And if Johnson's men didn't redouble their efforts to find them, it would be too late. They would find five heads on the end of five forks. That time, the president got the message loud and clear.' And Johnson got the rubber plantation.

But Johnson became a pastor in exile, and Taylor became the president. After the elections in 1997, which Taylor won with a comfortable majority (though a significant number of the voting population were either dead or exiled, and critics said the rest were bullied and terrified into the ballot box), there was an illusion of calm. Refugees came home. The international media left. And in undisclosed locations in Guinea and Côte d'Ivoire, the two new forces of LURD and MODEL hatched, broke out, and destroyed the peace. They had grown out of ULIMO-K and ULIMO-J, respectively, and they had, like the ULIMOs, no manifesto beyond removing Charles Taylor, even as Taylor's manifesto had been to remove Doe – and Doe hadn't even meant to start a coup. But they had enough weaponry and some discipline – not much though, as this is Liberia – and got to the gates of Monrovia. Actually, to the bridges, and specifically to New Bridge, where the boy now sells his red sweets. By then, Taylor had been isolated by arms and travel sanctions imposed by the UN under pressure from the UK, who were trying to stabilize Sierra Leone and Charles Taylor wasn't helping.

By mid-2003 LURD held Bushrod Island on the other side of the bridge, with its markets and Monrovia's port. It was a stunning success, helped along by US officials from the Department of Defense who were instrumental in playing 'a role in coordinating military and other activity designed to rid Liberia of Charles Taylor', according to the International Crisis Group. The indictment of Taylor by the Sierra Leone war crimes tribunal was a prod, too: LURD launched its first big attack on Monrovia the day after. Yet the US role didn't extend to doing anything practical: exactly as his father had done thirteen years before, in July 2003, around the time of the most awful fighting, George W. Bush sent 2,000 troops who mostly sat offshore, in ships that Liberians could see, but which wouldn't do anything for them. This was cruelty, particularly as a US assessment team had reported back a week earlier that intervention was possible and justified to avert a humanitarian disaster. And still the Liberians expected help, even after Marines stationed at the embassy were instructed to hand out brochures telling Liberians not to harass their soldiers. 'The government never understood,' a nameless Marine told a *Washington Post* reporter, 'that the only thing that would happen if Liberians came up to us is that we would be kissed to death. The whole thing is hugely heartbreaking. The fact that they still look up to us makes it even sadder. It makes you ache.'

Small America, as Liberians call themselves, came up against small-minded America, and small-minded won. Operation Shining Express, as some fool in the Pentagon had named it, stayed definitely offshore, and the humanitarian disaster went ahead, as it always had.

When I look at Liberia now, after most of these men were done with it (LURD and MODEL are now in the transitional government, and they got the jobs with the fattest pickings), I think of soup. Liberians like their meat and fish, and soup which doesn't have any is 'empty'. Empty soup has the right contours, it looks right, but there are things missing. So I look at Liberia, and I see a country with some trappings of state and civility – an Executive Mansion, where women visitors have to wear skirts and men have to wear ties, a constitution that still enunciates the hopes of freed slaves, who 'were everywhere shut from civil office; compelled to contribute to the resources of a country which gave [them] no protection; who looked with anxiety for some asylum from this deep degradation'. But it's a bowl holding together empty soup. Emptied soup.

At the IRC office in Monrovia, they're holding Happy Hour. It starts at 4 p.m. on one Friday a month. The one I attend in January is packed, because Nicky Smith has only been country director for three weeks, and it's happy enough. But after an hour, everyone packs up and starts to leave. I watch them go with some astonishment. Whoever heard of a happy hour that lasts an hour? 'They want to get home before dark,' an IRC employee explains. 'It's best.' I say, but there's peace now, isn't there? He says nothing, swigs his Club beer – a miracle, considering how often the Club brewery was looted – and looks at me. And his eyes say, 'For true?'

# 3. Basketball Graves

'The fact that you escaped death on a particular day does not mean that you will not die; you could even die the next day.'

(Homily by Dr X, *The News*, January 2004)

There is a church in Rwanda that is famous worldwide. In 1994 several thousand Tutsis were shot and hacked to death in the church in Nyarubuye, and their bodies were preserved as a memorial. The church was headline news.

There is a church in Monrovia that is famous in Liberia. Six hundred people – mostly from the Gio and Mano tribes – were shot and hacked to death in St Peter's church in Sinkor in 1990, and their bodies were buried under the car park. It was never really headline news.

The difference is the bodies. They are not visible, and there weren't enough. In Nyarubuye the bones of the dead are displayed as a memorial. But at St Peter's the memorial is a stone slab installed by President Charles Taylor, which pays great heed to Taylor's father Nelson, who was killed in the priest's house that day, and adds the other 600 victims as an afterthought. It also pays tribute to a pastor, apparently killed during the massacre, but actually alive and well – I know this, because he'd shaken my hand five minutes before I read of his death on the stone slab. The bodies are at St Peter's, but under two white stars painted on the concrete. One mass grave is under the car park, the other under the basketball court, where the kids who go to St Peter's school play. It takes a genocide to earn the world's attention, and Liberians didn't qualify.

My hotel was directly opposite, but I never noticed St Peter's. It was just a church, with a school where children went in blue uniforms, on the other side of a two-lane road which was actually four-lane, and almost impossible to cross. But when I asked about massacres, the IRC staff had directed me here. 'There were so many massacres,' said Sianeh, the IRC secretary. 'Most of them were hidden, in the interior, in the bush.' The only one that is still talked about and remembered is St Peter's, because Nelson Taylor died there, and his son didn't let the country forget it. And she told me I'd been sleeping a hundred metres away from two mass graves, all this time.

St Peter's current pastor is Thomas Paye. He was working in the interior at the time of the massacre, which is fortunate for him; his predecessor was killed with the other victims. We meet in his small office round the back, where they'd found dead bodies, too, on the morning after. He's in the bathroom when I arrive, so I read the Bible to pass the time. It's been years since I last opened one; maybe it's got more interesting. I read this verse from Luke: 'If thy brother trespass against thee, rebuke him; and if he repent, forgive him. And if he trespass against thee seven times in a day, and seven times a day turn again to thee saying, I repent, thou shalt forgive him.'

Thomas Paye isn't in the mood for forgiveness, not about this. From the force of his anger, you'd think he'd been in the pews. There is a ferocity to his speech, when we stand in the empty church, and he says, as if to a busload of tourists hidden behind the altar, 'You are standing in the building where 650 men, women and children were massacred on 29 July 1990. Military people came here on 29 July 1990, with AK47s, M16s, all types of guns, and they began to shoot at innocent people who had taken refuge here. When they ran out of ammunition, they used cutlasses, they cut at their legs, they sliced. You see the bullet holes?' I see them. Dark spots in the coloured glass. 'You see the blood?' I see it. A dark space on the marble floor. The marble is porous and they couldn't get it all out. If they took out all the pews, and I stood on the balcony and looked down, he says, I would see more dark spaces, quite clearly. The pews were replaced after the massacre, as was the roof. It had been shot to pieces, then left open to the elements. St Peter's is only a stroll away from the Atlantic Ocean, so the salt and wind had wreaked damage on the wood. The soldiers approached quietly along the beach before they attacked.

The windows are the same, though. The same coloured glass – quite expensive, and therefore hard to replace – as was in the windows when, at about 7 a.m. on the day of the massacre, they came to find bodies, still dripping with blood, hanging halfway out, because they had been trying to escape when they were macheted or shot.

Father Lee Cahill, an Irish missionary, was there later in the morning. 'I'd got used to gore, by then,' he says from the missionary headquarters in Cork, because he stayed in Liberia between 1969 and 2002 and saw plenty. 'I'd even got used to the smell of blood. But that scene was horrible. Horrible.' Bodies lying everywhere. Babies whose heads had been smashed against the walls in the courtyard. Women gang-raped and hacked. All the gore you can imagine. 'I want you to imagine it,' says Thomas Paye. 'It was a mistake to let the bones be buried. We should have preserved it. It should be a place of memory.'

Father Cahill was chaplain at the St Joseph's Catholic hospital, three-quarters of a mile up the road. In that three-quarters of a mile there were three or four checkpoints that morning. He calls them 'crazy checkpoints', and he calls the men who carried out the massacre 'lunatics'. But he calls the men who ordered the massacre, and all the other men who ordered all the other massacres, something much worse. 'They are gifted men, and their personalities got twisted, broken. I can think of no milder word to call them than satanic.'

The hospital's driver – 'a fantastic man who didn't know fear' – made eleven trips with his bus full of survivors, through the crazy checkpoints, until the soldiers shot his assistant dead, and transported him to the Executive Mansion. They were soldiers, not rebels. 'They were our army,' says John Dayen. 'They were supposed to protect us, and they were killing us.'

When I ask to meet a survivor of the massacre, Pastor Paye suggests John. It's the fourth time John has been asked to tell his story, and I feel bad at asking him to retell it. But he doesn't mind. He minded when a German charity used him as a poster boy to raise money and then never sent him anything for his pains. But he doesn't mind reliving what happened, because he can do nothing about it now. So he tells it calmly and purposefully, sitting in the wheelchair that he's had to sit in since the soldiers came in that Sunday morning and shot his legs to shreds, and since the Belgian doctors from Médecins Sans Frontières, working twenty-four hours a day at the Catholic hospital, amputated both his legs at the top of the thighs.

He was fifteen at the time. It was a bad time for the Gio, his tribespeople. During the ten years Samuel Doe had been in power, ethnic differences had come to be used to cause trouble. Before Doe, Liberia's sixteen tribes had lived together peacefully, more or less. They had intermarried, traded, mingled. They resented the Americo-Liberian elite, but that was the extent of ethnic strife. But Doe was Krahn, and so were his favourites and most of his army. Doe's former ally, Thomas Quiwonkpa, had been Gio, from northern Nimba county, and his supporters were Gio and the linguistically related Mano tribe. When Quiwonkpa failed in a coup attempt in 1985, Gio and Mano were hunted. They were massacred in Nimba county by the shock troops of Charles Julu. By 1990 they were being recruited in large numbers by Charles Taylor and his NPFL forces, so in Monrovia they were being hunted again. Door to door, day and night.

The week before the massacre, John Dayen's father had been murdered at his place of work at the port. His colleague was a Krahn man, and he had reported him – for the crime of being Gio – to the AFL, Liberia's constitutional army, but now a Krahn-dominated force. 'As I heard it,' John says, simply, 'they mutilated my father bit by bit to kill him. They cut him up.' So John and his stepmother and two sisters followed hundreds and thousands of other Gios and Manos all over Monrovia, and took refuge in a church compound. People were sheltering in churches all over the city. Some were sheltering in the UN compound, now the headquarters of LoneStar Communications, Liberia's surprisingly functioning cellular phone service, part-owned by Charles Taylor and run through Monaco. But John and his family chose the Lutheran church. They calculated that it might be safer, because it was the church of the diocesan bishop.

They stayed there for two and a half months. There were about 1,000 people, so they organized themselves: men and the older boys stayed in the church, women and children stayed in the church school buildings, right next to the church in the compound. It was OK for a while; NGOs would bring food, and they were relatively safe. 'There were some incidents, when AFL soldiers would come and try and capture people from inside the fence. There was one young boy – they told him to come over because they wanted to ask him something, then when he came they pulled him over the fence. Later we heard he'd been killed and buried on the beach.'

There was some safety, because of the US Marines. George

Bush senior had sent four warships in June 1990. Most of the 2,300 Marines stayed offshore, but close enough so Liberians could see them, and they stayed there before sailing off in August. Elements of a Marine Expeditionary Unit did come ashore to help guard the US embassy for a couple of months. Later, they were used to evacuate American citizens. No one else, because that wasn't US policy, however much the Liberians might have thought that US interests in Liberia should have dictated otherwise.

The Marines made themselves useful, before they left. They started patrolling around the church after the incident when the soldiers snatched the boy. They would advise people to stay away from the fence, to stay indoors after 6 p.m. to stay away from trouble.

But trouble was being planned. It was 2 a.m. on Sunday morning. By then, President Doe had passed a decree instituting a curfew. People thought it was to ban the Marines from patrolling, that it was to set the conditions for the massacre. It's probably true, because when the dogs started barking and the soldiers started climbing over the fence early that morning, there was no one to stop them. The men saw them through the stained glass windows, watched as they went to where the women were, broke into the storeroom, lined up the women, told them to give up all their jewellery and money. They took it, and left.

'No, actually,' says John. 'I forgot something. There was a woman there who had been sheltering in the UN compound when they tried to do a massacre there. They hadn't been too successful, and she'd been really critical of President Doe. So when they came, they asked for her, and they raped her and killed her.'

Gang-rape? 'Of course.' Anyway, they thought the soldiers had gone away, but then they came back, 200 of them, this time, with 'big big guys' that John recognized, though he was only fifteen. But he'd been paying attention to who was who, because his life depended on it. (On television one evening, I watch a programme about Abkhazi refugees. A man with no electricity and no running water, who has been displaced for twenty years, says wonderingly, 'I can't believe some people are so safe, they don't even know the name of their president.')

There was Charles Julu, nicknamed 'the butcher', and General Alfred Smith, who had led the massacres in Nimba county in 1985. John also thought he recognized a chubby man with an overgrown Afro and foolish mouth. Samuel K. Doe. 'The president was there. I saw him. He was just observing.' When the order came to shoot, it came from one of the big guys. Maybe the president, maybe not, but it was in Krahn dialect. They told the women to speak their tribe, and then they started shooting. Meanwhile, other soldiers came back to the church and told the men to open the door. They said no. 'We said, "You're already killing people, we're not going to open it." So they broke the front door, came in and started shooting.' People tried to escape but soldiers were blocking all the doors. Next door, in the school buildings, the women were luckier; they found a way out through the roof. Many escaped, including John's stepmother and one of his sisters. His elder sister was killed.

The children were with the women. 'So many were killed. They didn't shoot them, they would take the baby from the mother's back and knock the baby's head on the wall, to save ammunition.' They applied the same principle in the church, too, after a while. As well as guns, they'd brought machetes. They had come prepared.

'I want you to imagine it,' said Thomas Paye, and I try. Pitch black. Noise and screams. Men with flashlights, swinging their blades in all directions, shooting in all directions. After the massacre, people saw women and children with their feet and hands blown off. Thomas Paye thinks the killing lasted four hours. John thinks it was forty-five minutes. John's probably closer to the truth. 'I don't think it was four hours,' says Father Lee Cahill. 'They wouldn't have needed that long.'

While they were still busy on the ground floor, soldiers noticed the choir balcony. It was dark, and they'd had their backs to it, probably. This was where John was lying, partly hidden behind the organ. 'When they got through shooting, they told us we should come down. We said, no, we wouldn't. There was a lot of talking.'

Liberians are a conversational people, but there must be a limit. John doesn't think there's anything strange about negotiating your own death. 'They wanted us to come down and get in the truck. We said we could see through the windows that they'd been killing our mothers and sisters, and we could see our fathers lying in the yard. We said, if you want to kill us, kill us in the church.' And they did. 'They were just shooting, shooting, shooting directly at us. Fortunately for me, I was behind the big organ. Fortunately, because I'm still alive. But my two legs were out. So the gunshots damaged both legs.' One leg was shredded; the other nearly shredded. 'Twenty people were killed. So many of them fell on top of me. When I touched my hair, I thought it was my brain, but fortunately it wasn't mine.'

He's not clear what happened next. 'I was not to myself. Because of the sound and the powder, you know.' He doesn't remember screaming. 'Actually when a bullet touches you for the first time, you don't feel it. Anybody that you ask that has bullet wounds – the first moment, you don't know. After ten to fifteen minutes, you start to see your blood shooting out.' After they left he tried to get up, to look through the window. He fell down, and realized he had virtually no legs left.

There was nothing to do but wait. At 6.30 or so, the soldiers came back. John hadn't moved, because he couldn't. 'The commander of the death squad, Charles Julu, he came asking whether there was anybody alive, that he was here to take us to hospital. But we couldn't believe him. I was looking through the window, and I saw they caught one guy and they put him in the trunk of the car. I knew they were going to kill him, because if you want to take somebody to hospital you won't put him in the trunk.'

Later a man from the International Red Cross arrived, and the Catholic hospital's driver began his dangerous shuttle up the road, through the crazy checkpoints staffed by lunatics who were probably yawning from their busy night. John's stepmother escaped with her surviving daughter to an uncle's house on the beach near the church. They were afraid to be on the street, because anyone with blood on them was obviously from St Peter's and a target. Later, after the whole of the Catholic hospital had been evacuated up to Phebe hospital in Bong county, and before Phebe was attacked again – it was hit half a dozen times over the years – and John had to move again, he found his stepmother. Two people who thought they were dead were not. But John had no legs any more, because of the war, twice over. First, because of the shootings, and secondly, because the war was coming too close to Monrovia and the bones wouldn't have time to mend.

What remained of his legs healed, slowly, but he was in a wheelchair. Which made it tricky, in 1996, when he became a refugee, like everybody else. He couldn't exactly walk to safety, like most people did. 'I went to Paynesville and got transportation. I was scared. I never got used to what rebels did. I mean, I didn't care about the ones in Monrovia, after what had happened to me. But outside, I wasn't sure what they'd do.'

He got across the border safely, but he didn't stay long. 'I was in a house in Côte d'Ivoire and I saw a Liberian taxi. Someone must have chartered it. I burst into tears, I was so homesick.' He decided to come back, no matter what. 'Though war is in Liberia, here you are free to do anything you want to do. Compared to other countries in Africa, [where] you are not free to open a small business. You are not free to do anything, if you are not a native of Ivorian soil.'

And he stayed, despite everything. Despite running into one of the men who had blown his legs off. 'It happened once. I was visiting a friend, and there was a guy on the porch. I left, and the guy asked my friend, "Who is that guy?" He said, "One of the victims of the Lutheran massacre." And this guy said to him, "Oh, we all participated in that massacre." So I went back to visit him again, and the fellow was sitting on the porch. I just sat down and looked at him, and I thought, I will not bother him, I'll just forget about it. These people are not ashamed.'

Today John works as a receptionist at Handicap International. It's a scruffy building in the grounds of JFKMC, officially named the John F. Kennedy Medical Centre, but known by most Liberians as Just for Killing Monrovia Citizens. (ECO-MOG, in Liberian, stands for 'Every Commodity or Movable Object Gone'.) The Handicap International building is probably the only one in Monrovia with a ramp, and is full of ex-combatants. The day John and I meet, a young man is walking slowly up and down, following the same path, trying out his new foot. I think it must be hard for John, having to help fighters get better. But he has no time for my knee-jerk sympathies. 'It's my job. I register them and they get their prosthesis. They start talking about how they killed this and that and we tell them to forget about it, to just get on with their life.'

Now he wants to go abroad to get a computer degree, 'because there are too many people exploiting people here'.

But he has no money, like most Liberians. And it's hard to get qualifications here, when you can't get to the exam hall on time. 'Taxi drivers assume I'm an ex-combatant. They think ex-combatants won't pay the fare. And if you argue with them, you'll just prove you're an ex-combatant. I have to pay money upfront to change their minds.'

So he's late everywhere, all the time. It bugs him, but that's the extent of his anger. He's serene, considering.

Pastor Thomas Paye isn't. We stand by the basketball grave, which John doesn't like to visit, because he doesn't like to think he's wheeling over the bones of his sister. The children are making happy noise in the school; the classrooms are packed, and they're the privileged ones who can afford the school fees, and the dead bodies are under our feet, and we're standing on top of the past and in front of the future. Yet there is cause for pessimism about both, says Thomas Paye. 'There are three generations now. Our generation, who knew the virtues of society. The spoiled generation, with a culture of violence and war, and then there is the generation that will be following. We have to prepare for them. It's too late for the spoiled generation. Twenty-four years of conflict! It's impossible. Just impossible.'

# 4. The Rebel Business

**US IMMIGRATION INTERVIEWER:**
Why did you never take up arms?

**INTERVIEWEE:**
Oh, I was never active in the rebel business.

You will not see dreadlocks in Monrovia. Or bleached hair, or cornrows, or large Afros or bandannas. And if you do, you will know who you are looking at. Only ex-combatants wore their hair like that, and now that there is peace, most of them have had it cut, because most people in Liberia are talking and walking peace. Even so, when you drive around Monrovia, you can see the ex-combatants, because their walk is different. They're the boys with a certain swagger, with the low-slung American-style hip-hop jeans, with the tape recorders and ghetto-blasters. They're the ones with the hairdos, the bandannas, the Ali-G skullcaps. They're the ones who made money in the war. Other people's money. And they are the ones who know what their look symbolizes, and who refuse to change it. They are the shameless ones.

## Michael

Michael was a combatant. He knows exactly when he became 'ex'. It was when he cut his hair. He now wears the commonest hairstyle for young men in Liberia: short, nondescript, un-coloured. The natural look means something. Michael thinks it means peace.

We meet in Kakata, a sizeable town north of Monrovia. It's a Saturday, and Gayah from the International Rescue Commit-tee has been driving me round displaced-persons camps, where I have heard stories that are humbling and horrible. I am feeling dazed, and it's late in the afternoon, but we still have to meet Michael on the way back. I've never met an ex-combatant, and I'm curious to know what the people who did unspeakable things to people look like.

Michael looks like a fifteen-year-old boy. Which he is, and a four-year veteran. He fought for Charles Taylor's NPFL forces, and he says he was good at it. Now he lives in the home of a pastor in Kakata. Given IRC security regulations, it's just about the furthest place I can go in Liberia, short of hitching a ride with an UNMIL (United Nations Mission in Liberia) battalion. This was the first place that UNMIL soldiers deployed to outside Monrovia, and it was the site of their first battle. It's hard to visualize a battle here, because the streets only supply standard African scenes – people walking, people shopping. But only four months earlier there had been other African scenes – people running, people dying. Again. The rebels were apparently chased out by UNMIL, but Gayah says they still live here. How do you know, Gayah? Everyone knows! 'You take a taxi with some of the ex-combatants, and they tell you what they have done, and they are not embarrassed. They are never embarrassed.'

There are ex-combatants of all sorts walking the streets of Kakata. Everyone knows who everyone else is. People know who fought for LURD, and people know that Michael fought for the NPFL. Before we sit down to speak, in a small church across the track from the pastor's house where he's now living, a man wanders in carrying a plastic bag. His voice is hoarse and barely intelligible, probably from years of yelling orders. He says he used to be in the Anti-Terrorist Unit, who were Charles Taylor's most trusted forces. They were led by Taylor's nasty son Chucky, now in exile somewhere unknown, and as restrained a character as that other junior despot Uday Hussein. Chucky once shot his driver because he'd killed a dog. It wasn't even Chucky's dog.

The man freely admits to having been in the ATU, though now he works in the 'currency business'. This is appropriate, as those classic Nigerian fraud letters – 'I am the son of a dictator, but give me money to release my millions' – have now started arriving in inboxes with Chucky's name on them. Still, I'm not sure what the currency business means, and why it involves plastic bags. Maybe he is something like Yacouba, the cunning trickster and 'multiplier of bank-notes' who features in Kourouma's *Allah n'est pas obligé*. I don't ask, because I don't like this man. After he's left, Gayah says he gave him the creeps too. The ATU were known cannibals. Michael doesn't show any reaction at all.

He's a strange boy. A boy, not a man, he says, when I ask him which he is, even though he's been doing a man's job for years. He sounds like a boy, at least, the way he starts most of his sentences with a sweet-sounding, 'Ohhhh,' like he's oiling his brain before speaking, before going on to explain about killing and butchery. He wants to do training, to be a motor mechanic. He wants to disarm. He wants peace. I am sceptical, perhaps because his eyes bother me. I have read often of 'dead eyes', of people with eyes with no soul, and dismissed it as poetic rubbish. But I can't see anything behind Michael's eyes, and I can't imagine what they've seen, either.

There are no firm figures for the number of child soldiers who have fought in Liberia. The official current estimate is

20,000, out of a fighting force of about 75,000. Charles Taylor led the way, characteristically, when he formed his notorious Small Boy Units in 1989. The street-smart crook knew the advantage of small soldiers: they are good at games, and war is a sort of game, so why wouldn't they be good at war? He was right, especially once the child soldiers had been armed with drugs and drink, to make them brave, and with 'juju' magic charms and spurious initiation rites to protect them from bullets.

Initiation rites are respected in Liberia, where 'secret societies' for men and women are still honoured and practised, and still secret. Behind the Christianity and the Americana, old gods are still honoured and magic is respected, enough to be exploited. So a commander can say any charm is bulletproof, and a boy or girl can choose to believe him. The theory of juju seems ridiculous to me, but I've never been stuck on a blind bend, waiting for a jeep full of armed enemies to turn up and kill me. There have been reports of commanders firing blanks into their small boys and girls, to prove the 'bulletproof' power of juju. In 1996, when Taylor's NPFL fighters marched into Monrovia, one American colonel, standing on the embassy balcony, burst out laughing. They wore toilet seats around their necks, and carried insect repellents and broken power-drills, the cords still trailing, as weapons. He was laughing, because of the discrepancy between reputation and reality. These were the scary NPFL fighters?

But their material weapons didn't really matter. Filled with enough dope and drink, they didn't fear death, and this was their best ammunition of all. As a Hamas official once commented about Palestinian suicide bombers, that 'Jews love to live, and that is our advantage.'

Many children were coerced into fighting. There are numerous reports of rebels entering school compounds and telling the teachers to close school down, because the children would be better off at war. They weren't wrong, materially speaking. Job opportunities outside the army were rare, pay was low and haphazard. The rebel business was more lucrative than any other kind. In Sierra Leone and Liberia the rebel business was known as Operation Pay Yourself.

Allen Lincoln has seen plenty of people in the rebel business. He runs interim care centres for Don Bosco Homes, where child soldiers are supposed to become children again. 'So you have the war in 1990. Children who took up arms then, they are now twenty-three. They have known nothing but war. They have encouraged other children to come in, because war has been glamorized. The gun has been glamorized. You take a gun, you have power, you have everything. You can get a car with a gun, you can get a house with a gun, you can get a woman with a gun, you can get money with a gun. If you can get everything with a gun, why not stick to the gun?'

Michael is a war child. He was born in 1988, and the wars started a year later. So it's miraculous, really, that he didn't join up until four years ago, when his mates started giving him hell when they saw him on the street; they'd already joined up and it was good fun. No coercion was required. It was fun to fire a gun that's longer than your thigh bone. Fun, to walk into someone's house and take their clothes, their nightdresses and their toilet seats, the copper wiring and the solar panels. (By last year, Liberian car-owners had learned to dismantle their cars to make them 'looter-proof'. It was the only way.) Fun, to drink and steal and rape, and get high, and you can do these things all the time, whenever you want.

So, like any normal eleven-year-old, he disobeyed his parents, and like many eleven-year-olds in Liberia, he joined the NPFL. He hasn't seen his parents since. These days they are refugees in Côte d'Ivoire, because they had to run from the fighting that their son was partly responsible for. Now, he wants to be a refugee too. He traced them through people he knew, and he wants to go back to them. 'I think they'll be fine with me.' Liberians are good at forgiving, if the tales I am told are true. 'There is no bad bush to throw your child' is a Liberian saying. No matter how bad they are, they will never be rejected. In an IDP camp up the road from Kakata, a young woman called Marline had told me about her brother, who had joined some fighters or other – she doesn't say which ones, perhaps because they're all the same in the end. He came home one day with his gun, pointed it at his mother and demanded money. They gave it to him. Years later he came back and asked for money again, only without his gun, because he'd sold all his looted possessions. His sister gave him an IRC T-shirt, because he had lain on the floor and sobbed for forgiveness. 'I'd still help him now, if he asked,' she says, with a shrug. 'He's my brother.'

Michael seems certain of forgiveness too, though I'm not so sure. Allen Lincoln doesn't always see happy endings. Families are poor and stretched, and used to the absence of their fighter in the family. 'If he wants to come back, how will they feed him? They can't even feed the kids they have.' Some friends are afraid of him now, he says, because he was a fighter and they weren't.

'They start off aggressive,' a teacher with several ex-combatants in his class tells me. 'But you talk to them, and they calm down.' I wouldn't know how to begin. Allen Lincoln says you begin at the beginning. 'If they say their name is Rambo or whatever, then you say OK, that's your bush name. What's your real name? We're not in the bush, so we'll use that.' It sounds simple: as if disarming and demobilizing 20,000 ex-fighting ex-drug-addicts is merely a matter of careful conversation. It's not, of course. The US ambassador recently made the striking point that all of Liberia's reconstruction is linked to education, because without schools, they can't put the kids back into education. Without schools, the children get bored and realize they are poor, and compare this to when they were fighting and richer; they make the obvious choice. Last time there was disarmament in Liberia, after the Cotonou peace agreement in 1993, child soldiers put down their weapons for only a year or two, until they noticed how much greener the camouflage-coloured grass was.

So far, Michael hasn't changed his mind, though there are more employment opportunities around for active combatants than for retired ones: Liberians fill the ranks of the Ivorian rebel forces next door. There is fighting in the Congo and Uganda, and Liberia is the best marketplace for recruits. But for now, Michael's not interested, even though his fighter girlfriend Evelyn has gone back to her county, and he's not sure how to get to Côte d'Ivoire, and he's spent four years in a war whose perpetrators were not known for their patience.

His unit was called Jungle Fire. This was one of the more organized outfits, run by the unpleasant Benjamin Yeaten, a close personal friend of Charles Taylor and an undoubted war criminal. They were 300 people in the unit: men, women, girls and boys. It was a good place to be, says Michael, even if he wasn't quite sure what he was doing there. 'Dunno, really. Maybe because the war had attacked Gbarnga. I can't see them taking everything, attacking everything. Maybe I joined to protect them.'

Maybe not. In Kourouma's book, the precocious and clever small soldier Birahima is chillingly lucid, though he's supposed to be only ten years old. He sets off to find his aunt in Liberia, and joins up on the way, because it's cool, and it's safer. He switches from side to side with childish ease, and he sees what war does, and why it does it. And why, sometimes, there is no reason at all, and certainly not the one that the leaders pretend to have. *C'est la guerre tribale qui veut ça*, he says, like a curse. That's what you get in tribal warfare. Skulls on stakes, marking out the perimeter of a camp? That's what you get in tribal warfare. An eight-year-old girl, shot in the legs, left to be eaten by forest ants? That's what you get in tribal warfare.

Kourouma, who died in late 2003, saw right through tribal warfare. So does the Archbishop of Monrovia, who's supposed to be in the business of forgiveness, but seems to be finding it hard. 'This whole thing has just been a recycling of murderers and so-called warlords coming to redeem us. They rode on the shoulders of ethnicity. Ethnicity and religion are used for political ends, like the children were.'

It is a relief, to distil wars like Liberia's into easy explanations: 'ethnic hatreds', 'tribal warfare', 'crazy Africans', the standard 'heart of darkness'. But the truth is simpler still. Refugees have invented a new word to explain the wars, as they suffer the effects. I ask why Liberia is at war, and the response is always identical: 'power-greed'.

The complications are cosmetic. Liberians have been drowning in an alphabet soup of acronyms: PRC, NPFL, ULIMO, LPC, MODEL, LURD. 'There are so many!' laugh the people who have lost everything because of them. 'What does it matter anyway – they're all the same. A rebel is a rebel.'

War was very simple for Michael. 'I woke up and I drank, and then I could be active.' Active means killing people. It was an efficient tactic: Michael was good on the battlefield, right from the beginning. Training depending on how much man-power was needed at the front line, but he got two months, which was good. He started with AKs, and moved on to mortars, which he could launch by holding the weapon at knee height. It still fired OK.

He was a good shot, but his biggest strength was being well protected, because he had braided his hair. 'Oh!' he says, sing-song. 'If I had cut it, I wouldn't have been protected any more.' He had a couple of juju charms, too, and a piece of 'country cloth', the coarse material that Liberians weave. These were his 'bulletproof things'. He had his own weapon, and he wrote his initials on it. He wrote MS, his real initials, though by then he'd been given a proper fighting name by his commander. They called him Death Squad. He giggles when I ask why. 'Oh! I don't know. Because when I had to make moves, I made moves.' There are other children with more ludicrous names. If they weren't so lethal, they'd be funny: General Come-down-to-my-level, because that's what he made people do; Laughing-and-Killing, for obvious reasons; General Cairo Pooh-Pooh, because 'you can smell me but you can't dodge me' (which explains the pooh–pooh, but not the rest).

Some psychologists think such names helped children cut themselves off from their old life. They were Death Squad, so they weren't some mother's son. They were Cairo Pooh-Pooh, so they didn't have to remember their brothers and sisters, and so it wasn't really them killing someone else's. 'Liberians don't use first names,' a man tells me. 'You always refer to someone by their surname, so that if they cause trouble, you can always trace them back to their family.' The man's name is John, but he was always 'that Brownell boy'. If the child soldiers had new names, then they had new identities, and they couldn't be traced back. That's his theory, anyway. In reality, people in displaced camps around Monrovia know exactly who the fighters are, because they come and visit their families in the camps. I hear tales of women doing their chores, and spotting the boy who raped them, or killed their husband. One girl says she confronted her attacker, and he ran away.

Michael isn't ashamed of his name. Nor is he ashamed of what he did. 'I feel bad for civilians,' he says, fairly unconvincingly. 'Did I give civilians a hard time? They weren't the enemy. They are innocent. Did I see people doing bad bad things to civilians? Oh yes, I see some. For example, when we were walking from Gbarnga and civilians were retreating on the road and they can take anything from them! They can take money or tape recorders. It was bad! The thing is, it's only if you capture an area you can take things. You can loot.' There are pictures of child soldiers carrying looted teddy bears, small bicycles, child's things. They took money, tape recorders, light fittings. They took everything down to the dirty dishes. Michael doesn't deny it. Being a rebel is a licence to loot. Within reason. 'You don't see a person running and take a thing from a person. That's bad.'

Nor do I believe him when he says that he never took drugs, though he claims he only drank – beer, and local brews, and whatever was on offer. Drugs were necessary equipment: some commanders supplied their units with marijuana (known confusingly as opium), or 'bubbles' (amphetamines), or Nigerian tablets called dugees. Cocaine wasn't common (at least, outside the Executive Mansion, as the rumours go), but plain old gunpowder was, mixed with food for a cheap and appropriate high.

It worked for Michael. 'In my belief, I was brave. Some of them were scared to be on the [front] line. Some people in a week they only go two, three times. I go every day. There was nowhere else to go.'

He says he doesn't know how many people he killed. He only remembers a few that he killed face to face, because none of the parties in Liberia's wars bothered with things like prisoner of war conventions. If a soldier was big, he was killed. If he was a boy, he was killed or conscripted. If he was a she, she was raped then conscripted. Michael says he had no choice. He remembers one time he killed, near the bridge in Monrovia, during last year's fighting. 'It was World War Three. I'd been fighting and when I came back they told me that I had to kill an enemy fighter.' How did he know he was an enemy? What if he was just a civilian caught up in crossfire? Michael looks surprised. There are rules, stupid. 'He had cornrows! And cowries round his head.' Anyway, he knew the boy, since they'd grown up together in Bong county. 'He was blindfolded, so he couldn't see me, but I knew it was him.' There was no question of disobeying orders. I ask him how he killed him, partly out of indefensible ghoulish curiosity, and partly because I expect him to say he gave him a quick death, out of respect. 'I bayoneted him through the heart. It didn't take long. About fifteen minutes.'

For a moment, I stumble. I can't think of a question to follow that. I can hear the squelching and screaming of a knife being twisted. Then some strange objective logic sets in (the same way when, after two weeks of stories, a man tells me his sister was cut in pieces and I nearly say, 'How many?'). Michael had hardly been to school: how did he know where the heart was? But he was a soldier. He was prepared. 'They teach us that in training. They tell us, if you're shot on the right side, you might survive and if you're shot on the left, you'll die. I don't know why I didn't shoot him. I did not want to fire. Because of nothing, because of my own heart's desire. I did what I felt.' Not because it was quicker? 'Oh no. There's no easy death. If you shoot the person, you hurt the person. If you kill someone with a knife, you hurt the person.'

Michael's good at being the rehabilitated soldier. He cut his hair, because the pastor asked him to, and he talks the talk of peace. He's waiting for disarmament, and he wants the US$300 and the three weeks of rehabilitation and the training. Then he wants to go back to his family.

But he still has his gun, probably in his bedroom. He's not prepared to say exactly where it is, because I might report its whereabouts to UNMIL if he did. And he's not too happy. 'My friends are scared of me. They know I was a soldier and they weren't, so they think it makes a difference between us. They think I might harm them.' It's like a magic mirror. He looks in it and sees Michael. They see Death Squad.

## *Janet*

The media likes women soldiers. Especially butch, fighting ones. They like child soldiers too, for their cartoonish horror quality. When Osman Bah, an eighteen-year-old Liberian refugee in the UK, wrote about his time as a child soldier on a website, he was besieged with media requests. Nobody wanted to know about his time as a refugee, newly arrived in London and sleeping rough in Peckham. They wanted the glamour and the filth of war, not the tedium and dirt of asylum.

I am no different. When Gayah tells me there is a fighter called General Janet Jackson, I want to meet her. For her name and her reputation: she served in Charles Taylor's forces, and was in his personal bodyguard. She is an irresistible prospect.

Gayah arranges a meeting early one evening in the IRC offices. Two small people arrive, of indeterminate gender. One is wearing black-rimmed glasses and looks like a pocket-sized African Marxist or a Peanuts character. The other looks like a short butch dyke. This is Janet, and the Marxist is her half-brother Alfred. She's not a dyke, but she is butch: there is not much that's feminine about Janet, except she's a woman, and she's got a man and a child at home. She calls her man 'a civilian', because she's still a one-star general, though she's not in uniform, and her commander-in-chief is in exile. She's still on the payroll of the SSS, Taylor's Special Security Service, who were the presidential bodyguard and justifiably feared. I can see that Janet would inspire fear without much effort; she makes me nervous, although on the evening we meet she's equipped with only a mobile phone and her half-brother. Alfred has a careful manner, and he unnerves me. Especially when I ask if he was a fighter too. 'When you're in Liberia, you're all exposed to war in some way or other.' Yes, but did you fight? 'Well,' he says slowly, watching his words, 'I would say no. But we gave ideas, we shared things from the other side.'

Janet and Alfred sit side by side on the sofa, two short people with long histories. She has come to talk only because Gayah has asked her to, or perhaps because she expects money. When CNN interviewed her last July, when she 'held' Freeport, they paid her US$300. 'Look on CNN,' she says, animated for once. 'You will see me! They know me!' I do look, but I can't find her. There are stories about Black Diamond, the leader of the Women's Artillery Command (WAC), whose fighters were known for their blue hair gel and red nail polish, their high heels and fighting uniforms consisting of bikinis. Janet wouldn't have stooped to that, because she's a proper soldier. She's had training in Burkina Faso. Everyone knows of Janet here not because of her bikinis and heels, but because she lives in Paynesville, like Gayah, and she has a reputation. 'They all love me,' she grunts in her strong patois. During the fighting last year, she says she held the whole road between Paynesville and Camp Schiefflin, north of Monrovia. She says everyone loves her for it. I've yet to meet a civilian who confesses to any love of any combatant, but I'll let that pass.

There's so much talk of truth and reconciliation going on – tune in to the UNMIL radio station, and you are soon drowning in brotherly love and peace – that I'm probably being unkind or inappropriately curious – I've never met a female general, and I don't want to know what she thinks of reconciliation. I want to know what she did to help get Liberia to a point where it needed it.

Janet thinks of herself as a freedom fighter. She's very firm about this. Perhaps because, unlike a lot of women soldiers who have fought on all sides, she was not forcibly recruited, or abducted or raped, or turned into a 'cook' for the troops (being a cook meant providing sexual slavery too). She joined up voluntarily, because her girlfriends did. 'I was eighteen. I decided to help free our country from the Doe regime. We were freedom fighters!' A friend of hers had joined up in Nimba county. This was Charles Taylor's richest recruiting ground, because it was full of Gio and Mano tribespeople, who by now were hunted by Samuel Doe's predominantly Krahn militias, and who had been massacred by the troops of General Charles Julu in 1985. Janet was trained for one month at the Gbatala army base in Lofa county. (In an Amnesty International report in 2001, civilians reported being detained at Gbatala. They were beaten with bayonets and burned with cigarettes, then made to stand in holes in the ground, up to their necks, where they had to urinate and defecate.)

The instructors at Gbatala were South African. 'They were your colour. They were hard!' She learned how to fire, dismantle the weapon, put it back together, how to go into the front line, how to fight, the art of concealment. She was good in her training, but she was even better on the battlefield. 'I went to the front on 15 March 1990. We captured a town in the bush.' Did you like it? She laughs and so does Alfred. 'It was *baaad*.' She means good. Did you kill anyone? She laughs again. 'I don't know! Unless I see the dead bodies I don't know.'

When the NPFL invaded Liberia on Christmas Eve 1989, they were initially successful, even though Taylor had only 150 men. Taylor and others had been well trained in Libya, and they had anger on their side: Taylor's original fighters had been chased out of Nimba county by the notoriously vicious Charles Julu, Samuel Doe's most trusted soldier. 'When you are forced out of your country,' a refugee tells me once, 'and you are not allowed back, you will come back by force. That's not justifying what they did but that's why they did it.' And they recruited and recruited, because Samuel Doe had fractured the ethnic dimensions of his coup – the indigenous Liberians overthrowing the arrogant settlers – into dangerous proportions, so Krahn now hated and hunted Gio and Mano, and Gio and Mano hated and hunted Krahn.

Most fighters took fighting names. Anything to create fear, and to hide it. But Janet didn't bother with juju or magic, because proper soldiers don't. She just carried a pocket Bible in her breast pocket, and a practical short haircut. Even her fighting name is low-key. 'They called me Location Bee. Just because it was my radio call-sign.' No, no, says Alfred, who is quick to polish his sister's image when he thinks it's called for, in a way that I start to find creepy. 'It's also because it's an insect that moves around and gives people sting. It's because she's a strong lady.'

When I ask what Janet will be doing in ten years, she says, 'I'm praying for a long life,' but that doesn't suit Alfred. 'Actually, my prayer for her is to calm down and forget about these things and help her sustain herself.' Oh yes, says Janet. That's what she meant. 'I feel about it the way my brother talking.' I predict a brilliant career for Alfred as a government spin doctor, though perhaps he'd prefer the Church. 'She's my sister, I been all over with her, and all the time we been fighting, we been praying. In the whole part, she just does her soldier business.'

After a year on the front line in Nimba – when human rights reports regularly documented mutilations, rape, looting – Janet was promoted to major. 'December 14th. In the Executive

Mansion.' Her promotion was because she was better than the men on the front line. 'I was stronger than them. I was a strong fighter. And since I started fighting I never got wounded. Never.' Not long after, she was promoted to general. The secret to fighting, she says, is a voice of command. 'I encourage my men. If you don't encourage them, they won't work.' The secret to fighting is also fairness. There were rarely salaries. Commanders would be given money or loot, and the better ones would share it. Janet says she was always fair, and that's why no one deserted. 'If they wanted to [desert], I would say, "Gentlemen, what do you need? I will get it for you." '

Her gentlemen were actually mostly boys and girls. I ask Alfred how young is too young, for a soldier. 'The minimum age is seven,' he says, thinking about it. 'Yes, I would say seven. That's about right.' They volunteered, said Janet; how could she refuse them? There was no abduction, no forcible conscription, though I meet refugees who described NPFL fighters regularly coming into school and saying it should be closed down, and the children should go and fight. I meet refugees who have been raped with sticks and looted, but Janet must have been fighting a different war, because her troops were disciplined, and so was she. 'There was no raping! And if there was, they were punished.' How? She laughs. 'I know how to punish them.' She bought her troops' loyalty with fear and generosity. 'If I got any money, any food, I would share it. Some commanders didn't. But I did.'

The liberal conviction about female soldiers − if women ruled the world, it goes, it would be a safer place − is demolished by Liberia's wars, and by what women did to women. 'The women fighters were worse!' cries Satu Jalla, a woman who started running for her life from Lofa county in the early 1990s, and who is now living in Wilson Corner IDP camp outside Monrovia. She stands up and pulls her buttocks apart. 'That's what they'd do to you! They'd look for diamonds in there. They'd look for diamonds or money in your hair! If they see your pantie is nice pantie, they take it from you. They were wicked-o!' (The 'o' is Liberian emphasis, picked up from tribal languages.)

One woman soldier was called Equalizer, because she was there to equalize things. Another was called Pepper Bush. And the most fearsome of all was in Lofa, like Janet. 'She killed everywhere, more than anyone, so they gave her the name of Go-and-tell-the-war, because when she came, war was coming.' Even the non-combatants were to be avoided. A young man who spent a week walking through the bush to get to Côte d'Ivoire remembers them. 'The rebels had their girlfriends behind them, telling them what to take, what to loot.'

Janet insists her soldiers didn't rape. But she also insists that no government forces raped women, which is absurd. Some NGOs put the number of women who have been raped – by boys, by men, by sticks – at one in six of the population. Human Rights Watch considers the level of rape in Liberia qualifies as a war crime. When I ask women refugees if they know any women who have been raped, they snort with laughter at such a stupid question. 'Ha! There are so many, I can't remember!' When you are running, you are raped. That's life. That's refugee life.

Janet didn't tolerate this. 'I tell soldiers, if they kill a civilian, I kill you too. I shoot them.' I look disbelieving. Who was doing the atrocities, if not NPFL? Alfred takes pity on my ignorance. He explains, quietly and patiently, 'They had some groups called Strike Force. In that Strike Force they had a unit called Evil Forces. They used to do cannibalism, eat human beings. They had a reason. It was a kind of medicine. They capture any enemy, they eat him. Then when others hear your sound, they flee. It wasn't everybody, it was a special group. They were the most powerful group.' Later, I meet a young man from Sinoe county, also called Alfred, who was forced to watch a Krahn man being killed by Liberia Peace Council fighters. They cut off the man's head, says Alfred. They deliberately kept their knives blunt. Then they drank his blood. Really. I saw it.

I ask Marxist Alfred for more details. 'They weren't dead when they were cannibalized. Sometimes they would capture someone and tie you up and take your heart. The other guys, from ULIMO, they would use intestines as a gate. They would kill someone, take out the intestines and use them as a checkpoint.'

I lose my cool. I stare at him in disbelief. Do you think that's normal? He laughs. He's too sophisticated to believe in magic. 'Yes. You have to understand that there's a reason for it. If they do that, their credibility is bigger. They want to be in command. So whenever they get anywhere, the first thing they do is wicked things, so that when you see them, you will flee.'

It's getting dark now, and I'm feeling like I've stepped in something dirty. I want a large gin and tonic to drink away Janet's life, and her lies, and Alfred's demeanour, which is calm bordering on chilling. In their eyes a disciplined fighting force fought a noble battle, and it was fun. 'I love the sound of mortars! It's *baaad*, man.' Then she remembers it's peacetime, or maybe Alfred nudged her hard, because she backtracks to the platform of peace and reconciliation that all ex-combatants now claim to stand on. 'Oh, I mean, about the mortars, I feel bad for the civilians.' It pays to be contrite in Liberia, because people are talking of war crimes tribunals. If Charles Taylor's Nigerian hosts ever kick him out, he'll be sent to Sierra Leone's trial, and nobody's expecting loyalty. Certainly not the short and sinister Alfred. 'He's not a fool. If he's at the trial, he will get more people arrested. And they will all be Liberians and we will be losing good good people.' But personally, I say, are you worried about being indicted? Alfred laughs, and Janet grunts. They're not worried. Liberians have come to expect impunity.

When I visit Michael Francis, Archbishop of Monrovia, he jumps up five minutes into the interview, and fetches a photocopied newspaper cutting. He's got a pile of them, ready to hand out to visitors, and he gets very irate. The cutting is about a man called George Dweh, and accuses him, on convincing eyewitness testimony, of having his workmate Johnny Nah killed. The eyewitness is Johnny Nah's son, who was shot but escaped. 'I recognized George Dweh who my father had spoke to shooting from the front seat of the car. In a matter of a few seconds, the bullets were hitting my father all over, his legs and his two arms were broken, and I ran towards the swamp.' When Johnny returned the next morning, after a night in the swamp, he found his father's body, mutilated. His sister had been shot in the forehead. His mother, eight months pregnant, had had her stomach ripped open. Archbishop Michael Francis has no doubt about the truth of this account, and he has no problems with publicly accusing the man who did the murders, even if George Dweh, in the Accra peace agreement, was given the position of Speaker of Parliament. 'They are all the same people,' Liberians tell me. Warlords, then politicians, then warlords, then peacemakers. It is risky to pass judgement, in a country of fragile peace. Various representatives at the Ghana peace accords describe the factions lobbying for the best jobs. 'I'll be happy with a state-owned enterprise,' one general said. He probably got it. Peace never tastes nice, in the beginning.

Janet hasn't got anything though. She's still on the SSS payroll, but she's probably not getting paid. She's setting her sights abroad. Not too close to home, like Côte d'Ivoire, or

Sierra Leone or Guinea, whose rebels used to pay decent money for Liberian fighters: US$300–500 a month, Janet says, with bonuses for overrunning a town, and fixed contracts of employment. But she's worth more than that. She'll go to southern Africa, or even further. 'That's small money for me, because I know what I can do on the front line. My life is involved. It's worth $1,000 a month at least. It's worth a lot.' She doesn't see the irony.

## 5. Woman Da Wat?

'Fighting, killing, looting, rape, harassment, epidemic, hunger and intimidation are part of the everyday life of IDPs in Liberia.'

(Norwegian Refugee Council, September 2003)

One in three women was strip-searched during Liberia's wars. A hand down your pants, fingers in your pubic hair, groping for money – this was so standard, it was hardly worth commenting on. I remember lying sick in a hotel room in Jordan once, and the room service man ran his hands under my pyjama top, and it was four years ago and I still feel sordid. These women were stripped constantly. They even have a special Liberian verb for it: 'They naked me!'

The bush must have been full of women borrowing clothes from other women. No one I met had arrived with a change of clothing. If they had shirts, they were taken. If they had nice lappas, they were taken. Class and money were irrelevant. Mary Kamara, who has class in abundance, was strip-searched. As were Joanne and Grace and Cerue, and all the educated, middle-class women. There was no difference, to a rebel who looks at a woman and sees a lootable thing. A thing, only. 'If you met a child soldier,' says Grace, 'he was worse than an adult one. So unreasonable. So *rude*. They used to say, "Woman da wat?"' Mary translates it for me. 'It means, "What is a woman?"' and Grace translates it further. 'It means, what importance is a woman? If you say, "Eh, my son," . . . they would say, . . . "Woman da wat?" It means you're nothing. If they say that, forget it.'

Maimu camp looks better than I expected. I expected tents and tarpaulin, not little whitewashed mud huts, some decorated on the outside with handprints and religious slogans. It's good to see that these houses are solid and cared-for, but it's bad too, because it means that refugees have been here long enough to prettify them. Though these are, technically, not refugees – they have crossed no international border, so they are only 'internally displaced'. To me, this sounds like they have stomach trouble. In a way, they do. From Monrovia to Abidjan, refugees and IDPs want two things: security and no more 'bugger wee'.

It takes me a while to understand about bugger wee, because colloquial Liberian doesn't bother with most consonants. Like French, there are no discernible plurals, and most words are a guessing game. Bush is *bu'*, socks are *soh'*. And bulgur wheat comes out as *bugger wee*. For this reason, I'm usually provided with an interpreter. At Maimu, one of several camps in the town of Totota, the interpreter is Marline. She is more educated than the rest, so best qualified to understand my strange English. 'We understand Americans better,' she says, apologetically. 'They're more like us.' Sometimes, Marline's translation only requires her to move the intonation in the sentence. Sometimes, she needs different words. The question 'What do you do when you get your period in the bush?' becomes, 'What you do when you receive [and she raises her hands heavenwards] when you are runnin'?' She raises her hands heavenwards, because Liberians attribute everything to God, except war, but the answer is hardly divine: you soak your panties, and hope you can dry them out somehow, or you take a strip of lappa and use it as a pad. Ha! It's not easy! Sometimes Marline has to laugh at me, because there is no translation possible. 'Bugger wee – it's bugger wee! From WFP [the World Food Programme]. But we eat ri'!'

Rice is the staple food in Liberia. Swamp rice, normal rice; Liberians eat it constantly. It's some indication of the depths of their abyss that a country bountiful in rice now has to import it from China. Three weeks earlier, the UN had started distributing bulgur wheat instead, and the mutiny is still ongoing. The UNHCR (United Nations High Commissioner for Refugees) programme officer shrugs his shoulders diplomatically when I ask why an unfamiliar food is being distributed to a population dependent on rice, and asks me to stop my recording. I have read that it's an indication that rations are inappropriate when distributed food is sold in markets. Any market near an IDP camp is full of bulgur wheat. But the UNHCR man won't answer, except to say that the UN and the World Food Programme depend on the kindness of donor nations. Officially, they don't want to damage local rice production with competing imports. Unofficially, I suspect bulgur wheat belts in the US have something to do with it.

Either way, the bugger wee is unwelcome with the women, who do all the cooking. It makes their kids 'go toiletin' all the time. They want rice. They also want pots and pans, lappas and something to do. They want to do tie-dyeing, small small business. Anything! Being a refugee is like being at war: unspeakable excitement interspersed with unbearable tedium. At Maimu and Salala and Wilson and other IDP camps near Monrovia, there is nothing much to do except wait and talk. Though sometimes they need a little persuasion to do the talking part. Marline, faced with smiling silence, kicks off with her own story. She tells it fast, without emotion. It's just what happened. Like most Liberian stories told to non-Liberians, it requires a map.

'I'm from Gbarnga. The war came there in 1994, and we ran

and we went to Guinea. In 1996 we came back. Then in 2001 we ran away from Gbarnga and we went to Ganta. That was when Gbarnga fell. Then, in 2003, Gbarnga fell again and we were going to Ganta.' But the rebels stopped them, so they came to Totota, on 17 March 2003. 'Then when Totota fell, we were almost on the run, when the people were coming. The place was packed and everyone was set to run away, but where could we run? There was fighting in Totota, there was fighting in Monrovia. We were surrounded. It was not easy. People in the camp were afraid. Most of us had already packed a few rags that we take along. Just waiting for any alarm, we were going to leave. Everybody's bag was packed. But where could we go? Behind us, war there. In Monrovia, war there. Bong Town, war there. So we stayed here.' She stops, smiles, mentally brushes herself down. 'So that's how we are here. Anyone else?'

There is another pause. Liberians tell me that Liberian women don't like speaking about some things. Gayah, who is my escort around the camps, routinely gathers together a group of women to talk to me, then removes himself from the conversations. One day he leaves Peter behind, a Swedish IRC worker. 'I'm a Liberian man. They'll talk less while I'm here. An international is different.'

Not that Liberians are not chatty – they are, and pride themselves on it. Not like those close-mouthed Ivorians next door, or reticent Rwandans and Burundians. Liberians will talk about most things, at great length and with much laughter. But I am told they won't talk about sex, or rape, or things like that. Leymah Gbowee, who runs the Women in Peacebuilding Network, says there are still taboos. 'We have a big culture of silence. Women who have been violated carry it round for weeks and years.' WIPNET did a session a couple of years ago with fifty women. They just talked. Or someone just talked and the rest eventually followed. 'They sit there and think, My story is the worst. Then they listen to someone and say, . . . "Boy, I'm doing better than that!" . . . So then they can move on.'

In the early years of the war the blockage might have been semantic. 'They will say, "He slept with me," . : . or "He did something bad to me." Now, rape has become a frequently used term. Those that were gang-raped will say, "Soldiers came and took me." . . . One woman was bold enough to say five men slept with her one after the other. She was really unfortunate, because after they gang-raped her in front of her son, she decided she would come into town. Then there was a missile blast and half her face was cut off. She was hospitalized, and as soon as she was released, her husband left her. Really unfortunate.'

For a long time, health workers also didn't understand that a woman who said 'cook' meant 'rape'. Forced domestic service for fighters was rife, with the emphasis on service. Being a military cook was usually sexual slavery, with meal preparation thrown in. In one survey by Women's Rights International, over half of the 205 women interviewed had been forced to cook. On one bar graph, the two longest bars, for the question 'forced to cook and beaten/tied/detained/stripped/raped/attempted/sexual' are for 'stripped', and 'more than one type of'.

No one got respect in these wars. Not even Grace, Joanne or Mary: 'A woman like me,' says Grace, in her smart African-print clothes and jewellery, 'a middle-class woman, she would never have got raped before the war.' Now she would. At Salala camp, in the communal round-house next to the football pitch, I ask if anyone had problems when they were running. There is a chillingly soft chorus of *yeahs*. A young woman stands up suddenly and points to her belly. 'I still hurt here. I was four months pregnant, and they raped me.' She lost the baby. Her rapist was fifteen years old.

The IRC hands out GBV (gender-based violence) T-shirts with its workshops. The shirts are two for the price of one, and I see them during my trip, dotted here and there in a mass of people: a picture of a man beating his wife with a belt, and two versions of English, to save money. Liberian: 'Woman da your partner! Don suffer her!' Sierra Leonean: 'Woman not to slave nor mortal man like you!' They're conscious-raising, but they're also a change of clothing. It's debatable which the women find more important.

All the women know what GBV does, even if they don't know what it stands for. Some men know it too. A camp leader, sitting in his house – 'It's not a house,' he says, with a silent *doh!*, 'it's a hut' – mutters about Gender Balance, and the wisdom of putting illiterate women in charge of camp activities.

Why not? Fourteen years of war give you a PhD in organiz- ational skills. They have to. As Cerue of WIPNET says, 'The biggest problem is that most women are single parents. They lost all they have, they lost their husbands. They have to fetch for everything the family needs. Most of them don't have the skills required to have a good-paying job; they don't have the resources to do farming that would support the families. They don't have access to good medical facilities or good drinking water, so the children spend most of the time fetching water instead of studying. They don't have access to good communi- ties. Society has been rid of all the good behavioural norms. Most children are growing up in a loose community. So women are faced with *all* the challenges.'

At Maimu, Bakuu Mulbah wants to talk. She's forty-nine. Since 1999 she's lived in Zorzor, Gbarnga, Nimba, Kari, Totota and Maimu. I don't think she's ever counted them before, because it was always a provisional total, never final. In humanitarian language, Bakuu Mulbah has undergone 'multiple displacement'. In plain language, her life has been comprehensively removed. Except for the living and breathing part of it. Everything else – house, identity, self-sufficiency, security – has gone. 'They shoot you with a gun. If you have anything good, they take it from you. If they like your slippers [flip-flops], they take it from your feet. They take it, they rape you.'

Were a lot of woman raped? There's a chorus. 'Ha! We can't remember how many. Babies, women, old women. Everybody.' When 60,000 displaced people placed themselves in Monrovia's SKD stadium last year, the NGO Concerned Christian Community (CCC) did a quick survey. Of the 1,502 women registered with them, 626 had been raped. Or, 626 had been raped and admitted to it.

But can a woman tell her husband about it? There's laughter. 'But they do it in front of her husband!' A chirpy woman in a Robin Hood hat wants to talk. 'It happened to me. They made my husband watch. It was during the time we were crossing the river. It was only one rebel though. It only happened the one time. My husband was very vexed, but he was at gunpoint.' For good measure, they shot her brother in the face, too. 'We carry him to Guinea. But in Guinea, they stopped us, they said there was fighting in Liberia and we were involved. We said we weren't fighting. So they said they had to kill him. They said we had to pay 1,000 Guinea francs for them not to kill my brother.'

I ask whether anyone in the camp isn't traumatized. 'We all got problems! Isn't that so? The degree is unmeasurable.'

Some NGOs have tried to measure it. Two weeks before, WIPNET had started a workshop called Shedding of the Weight. It was very simple. Sit and talk. Leymah Gbowee, WIPNET coordinator, is not easily shocked, but she was this time. 'Out of twenty-three women from displaced camps, eight were violently raped during the last crisis, twelve watched a family member being killed, and the rest of them watched distant relatives being killed. Honestly, I was shocked. I couldn't believe that kind of evil. Then you're looking at them and a lady saying that her four older kids sat by and watched these teenagers rape her and her daughter.' Another woman's story: they tied a knife to the end of a gun and inserted it into her vagina. They told her that their private parts were too decent to use on her so they were going to use the knife. 'Even in the session now, she wears a pad all the time. She's bleeding and she's in severe pain on and off. This is from June, July. She didn't give the specific time because when they are telling their stories they are mostly in tears.'

I saw no tears. I saw laughter at what you'd think were inappropriate moments, but they're not. 'Sometimes when you go to these women,' says Grace, of WHDP, 'and they come up and say, "Yes, I was raped," or gang-raped, you'd almost think they were lying, because of how they tell the story. They're so calm, they're laughing, you would think it wasn't true. But it is true.' She tuts, African-style. 'We are a very peculiar people, Liberians. A lot of people will never be able to understand how we can laugh through the worst. They will launch a rocket and ten, twenty people die and thirty minutes later, people will be looking for the humour in the situation. That's the way we've been able to carry on.' She thinks it comes from the free slaves, some sort of genetic resilience. 'But I think we have taken it too far, to the point of complacency. We don't take anything seriously. We will laugh through any situation.'

They laugh when I ask them how you wash in the bush. They say it very slowly, all together, as if to a stupid person: 'NO SOAP!' They see that they can't explain properly how things were. When they say, 'We had nothing,' they see that I don't understand how much nothing that is. It turns out be a whole lot. No socks, no slippers, no soap. No clothes to wear. 'Like we were just born naked!'

## Market Woman

*(short story compiled from true accounts by the Women's Health and Development Programme)*

There lived a thirty-year-old woman called Markplay in Monrovia. The name Markplay means 'woman's behaviour' . . . Things went well until the war hit Monrovia. The house Markplay and her family lived in got destroyed. So she moved following the crowd with her husband, children, niece and mother. The little money she had, she put in the diaper and pinned it on her youngest child. That's how she was able to carry her money to Fendell. At the first checkpoint on the way to Fendell, a soldier grab her and said, 'Ay, you Dingo [Mandingo]?'

'Leave me, man. I look like Dingo to you? You ever see a Dingo wear jeans?'

'Then what's your tribe?' the fighter asked.

'Congo Bassa,' she said.

'If you sure you Congo Bassa then speak Bassa for me.'

While she and the soldier were exchanging words she saw another soldier grab a man who was ahead of her, pull him out of the line, carry behind the house within sight and shoot him to death. Then Markplay yelled, 'Oh my people!'

'What's wrong with this bitch?' said the soldier. 'That's how we will kill all you dogs.'

Then Markplay said, 'Da you dog, da your ma, dog. Come, let's go.' Markplay kept throw insults at the soldier until they left. That's how they managed to get to Fendell.

One morning Markplay and four other women decided to go to Kakata to buy goods to come and resell. On their way to Kakata they reached a checkpoint and Markplay was in front of her friends. The soldier shouted, 'Ay, you women go in there and let them search you.' She went inside. 'Take off your clothes,' said the soldier. She took off all except her slip and panties. 'Take off you slip and panties you fool,' said the soldier.

'I have my period,' Markplay said trembling.

'We know you women can lie too much. I want to see that period. Period tha what!' said the soldier. So Markplay took off her panties and the money fell. 'Ah hay! I see the period-o! This period is for me. You can go now.' The soldier was happy. And that was how the money she had used to disguise as Kotex was taken away from her.

When it was the second woman's turn, the soldier said, 'You, you for me. Hay! Small soldier, carry her to my house.'

The small soldier clicked his heels together and said, 'It for you, sir.'

After she was taken away by the small soldier, the commander of the gate came and release the other two women, but the second woman had already been carried to the soldier house and was left behind.

(Of course the soldier knew she was lying. Who can afford Kotex, these days?)

About 100 government fighters fleeing the rebel advance sought refuge in one of [the four camps surrounding Totota] on Sunday night, provoking panic among the inhabitants. 'The fighters entered the camp with their weapons – AK47s, grenades and other automatic guns. It was traumatizing for the displaced people living here,' Esther Washington, the camp protection officer told IRIN. (IRIN, 26 August 2003)

The women at Maimu take me on a tour of the camp. 'It's a lot less crowded now,' they say. It seems well populated to me, as there are more than 30,000 living in all three Maimu camps, according to UN food distribution figures – though these can be inflated by host populations signing up for food, because the IDPs get food and they get nothing, and they're not much better off. Who wouldn't sign up? But last summer, during the World Wars, 80,000 people were living here. In September, when there were rumours of shelling north of Totota, most of the 80,000 set off running again. The population of Salala camp, a few kilometres south on the Monrovia road, tripled, from 30,000 to 90,000 in two days. And this was after the ceasefire.

Camp and refuge are two concepts that should meet, but often don't. A static, unarmed population, in a clearly defined area, with no money, much frustration and not much protection: it's a perfect scenario for recruiting and looting. Fighters were abducted from IDP and refugee camps all over Liberia. So were women. Some camps became virtual military encampments, like Peace town in Côte d'Ivoire. A US State Department guide on how to protect refugees instructs staff to look out for obvious signs of militarization, like 'a long line of men marching in single file towards the border'. Other clues would reveal military activity: men taking food rations from women and families; a sudden increase in wealth; increased banditry; unexplained deaths; the refusal of some refugees to be housed in a camp; an outright military raid, or a strong rumour. After the 80,000 residents of Totota fled down the road from Salala, because they'd heard fighting was on the way, the fighting never actually arrived. But it easily might have done, and that amounts to much the same thing, when you're calculating your own safety, and when you live in a camp where protection is scarce.

Protection is the core mandate of UNHCR. That includes

the urgent stuff, like sinking wells and getting fresh water and sending tents and food. But it also means keeping the refugees alive after you've figured all that out. For years there have been discussion documents arguing about what protection is and how it should be delivered. Garmai Mulbah can sum up the need for it without documents: 'There was a case where they killed everybody. My sister, brother, her husband. A whole generation killed in one day. Why? Because they were travelling.'

'Uprooted from their habitual environment, the internally displaced remain among the most vulnerable groups in most conflict situations and are often deliberately targeted by government forces or rebel groups.' (IDP Project, Norwegian Refugee Council)

Refugees are prey. Yama Kolu, a fifty-five-year-old woman, illustrates this with the story of the snake.

'We went to Guinea. I was having my last child, and my husband went to get medicine. They captured him. They said, "You people go to Liberia at night and then you come here."' Rebel commuters. They took him to a police station in town; Yama followed, until they beat her so hard the baby fell from her back. They put him in a jail they'd built with rocks, and they put a snake inside. I say, 'Pardon?' She says, 'They use a snake! They put him inside then they talk to the snake, and they say, "If he's a bad person, bite him."'

Yama's husband was lucky – he was moved to a jail where the door was made of broken bottles, but it was snakeless. He stayed there for four months, and Yama couldn't do anything about it. She was a refugee without an ID card, and that was equivalent to being nobody. 'You had to pay the camp master 500 francs for an ID card, and I had no money and no food.'

Eventually, she went to see a local chief, and a complicated matter became very simple. 'I told him that we were refugees, that we were not here to fight. He said, "You sure?" I said, "I sure!"' The husband was released, and Yama's problems were reduced by one. Now she only had twenty-two dependants to feed, and no way to do it.

When you are the most vulnerable of the vulnerable, having access to food gives you protection. You aren't forced into unpleasant ways and means of finding it. The boys and men are vulnerable too, in a different way: they can get abducted or shot. The women suffer sexual violence and coercion. Single mothers and separated children are unprotected. There are posters all over Monrovia and the camps, dozens of headshots of children who have lost their families. Every displaced person knows about the International Red Cross tracing facilities, just as they know the words 'IDP' and 'refugee', and the difference. People stand at the posters, checking, with the intent of a jobseeker in front of a job advert. I see huts in the camps that use them for wallpaper.

There are hundreds, probably thousands of children living with families they don't belong to. Sia, who lives in Totota camp, but should live in Lofa, has a new son because of war. 'There was one girl, they stuck a stick in her, all the way up her. We took her to hospital, but she didn't make it. I got the boy now. He's eighteen years old.' They take in neighbours, nieces, nephews, strangers.

But they can't take in everybody. And there aren't enough men to go round, for protection purposes. In these camps 'child-headed households' are unremarkable. Female-headed households are normal, now that women comprise 75 per cent of the population. A household with a father would really stand out.

## Women in the High School

*(short story compiled from true accounts by WHDP)*

Women and war! Women in war! Women during war! School girls during war! Which ever way it is written or said, is an event that leave scars on the mind of any woman who has experienced war. Women's role during war is another experience that cannot easily be forgotten. Who knew what Liberian women were capable of doing? Who recognized our role? It was always said that women are 'weak and slow', but the opposite surfaced during the war when men were eating breakfast, lunch and supper under the bed, their hiding place. Women from all walks of life – school girls, old, young, executives – were the only peaceful people out in search of food to feed their families. Those men not hiding were out looking for women like fish lost in water. Those with guns were running behind young girls like children running behind children for feast. I tell you woman see trouble, yah-yah Liberian women experiences will be talked and written about until the end of life of Liberia. Please pay attention to this story. It is about events that happened to high schools in Monrovia during the early years of the war. The names mentioned are not true so don't feel bad if my character and you have the same name.

Long before the war high-school girls' school fees were paid by their fathers, but now it is not easy, the load is left on mothers and other family members like in Mondaymar's case. Her father supported her fully, provided all her wants and needs. She lived in her parents' house. Her father built a house and furnished it for she and her siblings along with their mother. He lived and worked outside Monrovia, but visited them regularly. Her mother, though not educated, managed the home in a civilized way. She always planted beautiful flowers around the house. Her mother was always engaged in making some kind of market but on very small scale but was always mocked by her daughter Mondaymar. 'Ma, you like money business too much. In city like Monrovia you are making waiter market in front of the house. What is it so much in small market, it is just waste of time.'

'My daughter, this small waiter market will help us to get salt and pepper money. Even your recess money come from this table market,' said her mother. 'Your father is doing everything possible to make us happy but I too have to help.'

During recess one day at school, Mondaymar and her usual group of friends were conversing about the war. Ellen said, 'We keep hearing about war in Nimba county, what is this all about?'

Muna said, 'Don't worry, the government will control the situation.'

'Control what situation?'

'We hear the soldiers are misbehaving in Nimba,' said Amy. 'Our next-door neighbour's relatives came last night from Nimba, about twenty persons.'

'Their stories are horrible,' said Maybel.

But they say the rebels are nice, they don't harm people. They are only looking for government soldiers. But they never saw rebels with their own eyes. For me, to God in heaven I want these rebels to get these soldiers from our back. Yesterday's newspaper had heads of beheaded men. These soldiers are bad. Look Maybel, I think some of these soldiers are rebels, that slim bright girl in the eighth-grade class – her father left this country during Quiwonkpa Coup. I saw him last week. Where is he coming from?

'He was one of the coup plotters,' Mondaymar said.

'Look Mondaymar,' said Ellen, 'as for me, I don't trust the government again, they lie too much. Let these new people come and save us. These monkeys need to go back to the forest of Grand Gedeh and hunt bananas and not human beings.' Let's go to class, recess is almost over, all this war talk will not make us pass chemistry.

The air of war gets closer to Monrovia. Some parents are afraid and have taken their children out of school and sent them to neighbouring countries. Two of Mondaymar's friends have left for other countries. Some days school, some days no school. No water, no light, no gas, no car. Food getting scarce on the market. Even dogs were getting scarce because soldiers kill them because of their barking.

Monrovia streets are deserted. Only army jeeps and trucks plying the streets. Heavy fighting in Paynesville. People are even afraid to sleep in their homes. More displaced camps are created in church compounds. Confusing movements of people. Some going to Graystone compound, others towards Paynesville, while others going towards Bushrod Island. No more communication between Mr Weager and his family in Monrovia. They are worried about his health. He is a pressure patient. He wrote a week before communication blocked requesting for reserpine tablets (pressure pills) because he only had five pills left. His wife tried several times to hire a taxi, three times but she was turned back. She told the last driver, 'My son, if you succeed tomorrow, please take these pills to my husband, he needs them urgently. I have to go back home and find food for my children.'

'Oldma, if I even succeed to go tomorrow, I'll only stop in Barnesville. I hear the rebels are around Johnsonville not far from your house.'

'Ah God, my husband, my children, how will I manage?' Tears rolled down her cheeks.

That day when she returned home, news came that rebels had taken Caldwell. Fighting between government troops and rebels escalated. One evening Mondaymar and others had to leave the house because one of the government shells hit the house and destroyed it. So inexperienced, only used to a few high-school friends, confused, no sense of direction, she did not know where to go. They walked towards Pipeline Road in order to take the bypass and get to Johnsonville where her father live. They were about seven in number from her house: her mother, her eighty-years-old aunt, two sisters, two brothers and her epileptic cousin. It was three days' journey to get to Pipeline Road. Rebels were all around like ants; all dressed in unbelievable manner. No news yet from her father. She saw her friend Ellen carrying her grandmother in a wheelbarrow. The tension was so high, they could not converse. 'Lord help me, my grandmother is dying. What is this? I think the monkeys are better than these so-called liberators. No hospital, no food. This old lady will die in my hands.'

Life on Pipeline Road, the events, the rebels, the stories, hard time, you name it. Mama said, 'Mondaymar, let me ask you something, you able to make market? My daughter sit down, you small girl. I don't want you to go amongst these people. You are too small.' She convinced her mother to give her a trial. 'My child, since you want to try, you can go ahead.' Mondaymar took five cups of rice from the bag. Rice was like gold dust at that time. With the twinkle of an eye, the rice was finished. Mondaymar got so much more money than expected. Ma, she said, God is really on our side, tomorrow I'll go to 'Kuwait market' to buy goods.

Day after day she got brave. Selling between fighters and soldiers. Her business really grew when ECOMOG took over Monrovia. One morning on her way to buy goods she met some fighters. They told her, 'Halt! Come here!' Cold sweat covered her face. If you move, pieces. She lost her voice for some minutes. 'Talk! We hear you girls are loving to these new soldiers who come to fight us. One thing we know, all of them have AIDS so, for you to not bring AIDS to Greater Liberia, we kill all of you.' At that moment she felt death not too far from her. Just about to talk, the fighter said, 'Shut up! Look at her mosquito legs. Go!' She walked like someone who has been in sick bed for days.

Mondaymar met Muna, one of her close high-school friends in the market. Mondaymar said, 'You know our own crowd of boys were holding guns or hiding. What turned me against gun men was the manner in which I saw them kill my mother's friend. It is still fresh on my mind. That morning, she was called out line to be searched. Her four big boys and two daughters standing around and looking; I can't forget the scene. She was accused of being a rebel supporter. "You rebel supporter," said the soldier, "we saw you marching that day but all of you will not live to tell the story."

' "My son," she said, "that na true. I don't even go among people. Please don't kill me, I have plenty children. Only me supporting them."

' "Close you mouth," said the soldier. "You think I don't know you? Pass in front of me."

'She started to plead again. "My son, please don't kill me."

' "Look you woman," said the soldier, "I am only waiting for the red pickup. In fact, tell your children goodbye. Talk!"

'She was saying, "My children, you take care of one another, oooh, that God will . . ." She was in tears . . . "tell my brother to . . ." Then suddenly the soldier fire her in the chest. My friend, that woman dropped, rolled and pulled grass until she died.'

No way to cry. The two friends parted and said goodbye. Mondaymar went home thinking about all the fun they had in school before the war. The war experiences kept coming and going in her mind. No condition is permanent, life can really change.


Bakuu Mulbah is from Voinjama in nothernmost Liberia. She hasn't been back there for years, but she hears things. And I am not allowed to go there, for security reasons – no UNMIL, no go. In its heyday, an AFP reporter wrote in 2001, 'the provincial capital was among Liberia's five largest towns and had its own radio station. There were five high schools, several elementary and junior high schools and scores of companies and private manufacturing units. The Tellewoyan hospital, the largest public health centre in the area, is today a sprawling concrete shell with no roof. A three-storey local administrative building – barely a few hundred yards from the hospital – is also in ruins. The walls of the building sport bullet marks. There are no doors or windows. The furniture was pillaged years ago.'

I ask Bakuu what is left. 'Ha! Everything is down. Everything is bushes. No villages, no business. No houses, no nothing. Everything is broken. We ask NGO to help us get back there, to build things again. But they have to help us.'

Liberians are self-sufficient and proud. They had a func-tioning country, a decent economy. Their land is rich in minerals, and it is fertile. Lining up for bulgur wheat handouts is humiliating, especially in the planting season, when you had rice fields at home. By now the fields should have been cleared, but nobody can get to them because the rebels are still in the way. At least there are few landmines. Liberia's wars weren't like Angola's. The wet tropical climate makes landmines unsuit-able – except for the remotely detonated kind – and there are reports that Taylor's allies in the RUF had bad experiences with landmines during their training in Libya. It's perverse to call Liberians lucky, but in respect of landmines, they are.

'I have a warehouse packed with food,' a woman tells me. She uses the present tense, though the food and the warehouse are long gone. Liberians use the present tense to describe dead people too. They say 'my father is a mason', when he was killed by a mortar shell thirteen years earlier. They have no time to gather photos or family mementoes. The present tense keeps a memory going.

There are gardens in some camps. Some are organized, down by the swamp. Some are little patches here and there, wherever the land is hospitable. 'There is no space,' say the women. 'Living here you facing people all the time, and there's no space.' The swamp land goes to the first arrivals, and they got here years ago. I take a walk to the swamp with Gayah, who thinks I'm weird to want to look at vegetables, but I think he's weird to enjoy stringy antelope stew, so we're quits. The gardens are divided into plots. Supposedly, the plots are divided fairly between families, but a young man at the gardens waves his hand at a wide area and says, 'That's all mine.' I would be suspicious of him – how does one young man have the power to have so much garden? – but he's reading a book about peace building, and I leave him be. Also, there's a boy in a bandanna and nice jeans walking around, and I don't like to disturb boys in bandannas and nice jeans. You need money to buy them, and the commonest way for a young man to get money has been through a gun.

The commonest way for young women to get money is the age-old way. The gardens are relevant, because a garden means food. So does prostitution. If you have one, you don't have to countenance the other.

In 2002 the UNHCR and Save the Children released a shocking report. It was shocking because it condemned their own staff, as well as peacekeepers, teachers and pretty much anyone in a position of authority in IDPs and refugee camps. From interviews with 1,500 adults and children in Guinea, Sierra Leone and Liberia, the report outlined allegations of abuse against sixty-seven men, in 'UN peacekeeping forces, national and international NGOs and government agencies for humanitarian responses'. These are the people who should keep you safe and fed.

In the report a Liberian child defined 'exploitation': 'When them big man go loving with small girl for money. Them big men can go loving to small girls, they can call girl when she walking along the road, and then the girl go and they go in house and lock the door. And when the big man has done his business he will give the small girl money or gift.'

Most allegations involved men in power trading humanitarian aid for sex. Oil, bulgur wheat, tarpaulin, ration cards, education courses, in exchange for sex with underage girls. This is just an extension of war behaviour: girls would take fighter boyfriends or husbands, for security and food. They were called 'security boyfriends' or 'bush husbands'. In the camps the same principle applies.

Sometimes the girls were living alone, or were the heads of their family. Often the family was complicit. You see a girl walking away with tarpaulin on her head, you know how she got it. I see a girl with shiny red shoes one day. She is pretty, and I wonder where she got the money for them. 'Oh, they cost nothing in the market,' an NGO worker said. But there's nothing and nothing. Most of the time it's impossible to earn even as little as his 'nothing'.

The complaints about bugger wee suddenly become less humorous. If food for thirty days runs out after ten, there are few options for survival. Families with gardens can eat; families without cannot. The UNHCR team reported very obvious teen pregnancies in camps. 'If we had alternative ways of making money,' said a teenage refugee mother in Guinea, 'I would never look at another man again for a long, long time.'

When you become a refugee in Africa, you lose a lot of social security. Extended families are protection. Young girls without them are prey. They don't even have friends. A girl mother in Guinea: 'The adult women treat us as children and make us feel we do not belong to their group. The young and single girls of our age who have no children make us feel we dirty because we did something bad and they feel if they are with us the men will not like them, so they do not like us any more. We are lonely most of the time.'

★

There are no gates on the IDP camps I visit. There are hardly any UNMIL patrols. There is no surprise in a place like this that a rumour is enough to make people run in fright, as they did last year. Physical security is a core right of refugees, but it's harder to deliver than bulgur wheat. The young woman who was raped by a fifteen-year-old boy is not allowed to forget it. 'He comes here, to see his parents. He hides from me, because he knows what a bad thing he did.' She wants to ask him why he did it, but he always runs away. She's stoic though, because she has no choice. She will watch and wait, just as all the women are watching and waiting until they can go home. There's no question of going anywhere else. 'Look, if someone wants to carry me to America, I'll go,' says one middle-aged woman with a grin. 'But I'm happy to go home, too.' 'I came back to Liberia early, when I was a refugee,' says another. 'I came back before anyone else. Because it's my home.'

Now they're waiting for Blue Helmet salvation, and a lift. 'UNMIL have got to Gbarnga so we're more than happy. But it took three months to walk here; we're not walking back.' But they will if they have to. They want to travel, but only homewards. None of the women wanted to go to America, or abroad. Why would they? It's not home. 'I came back early one time, from being a refugee,' says one woman. 'Why? Because it's my home. There's nowhere better.' But there's nothing there, I say. 'We'll build it. It'll be all right. We just need some help.' And a lift: it took all those months to walk from Lofa, they say, and they don't intend to take as long to walk back. They'd rather hitch a ride home, with the help of 'you people'. As soon as the Blue Helmets get to Lofa, they say they'll be off. 'And when we get there, we'll have a party. We'll have a bulgur wheat party. Bugger wee-o!'

# 6. Job Title: Refugee

Refugees should receive at least the same rights and basic
help as any other foreigner who is a legal resident, including
freedom of thought, of movement and freedom from torture
and degrading treatment.

*(UNHCR Basic Facts)*

On the blackboard are the four basic principles of refugee
protection. They are: Physical Security, No Refoulement, Basic
Rights and Durable Solutions.

The class notes them dutifully in their books. They ask for
the English translation of *Refoulement* (forcible return of refugees
to their own country), but otherwise, they know all this already,
because this classroom is a Lutheran church in Côte d'Ivoire,
and the students are Liberian refugees. In every sense the teacher
is preaching to the converted. On the sign-in sheet that is
handed round, there is a heading for 'job title'. Some have
written 'chairlady' or 'teacher' or 'prayer lady'. But most have
put their full-time occupation, because they have been deprived
of any other. Under 'job title' they have written 'refugee'.

Simon-Pierre is the teacher today. He's an Ivorian education
officer for IRC and, with another half-dozen IRC workers,
he has come on a bumpy car ride from the Tabou office,
down red dusty roads through green palm plantations, to Nero
Village. This workshop is about protection, because protection
involves ensuring the safety of refugees at risk. These Liberians

live in Côte d'Ivoire, and so they fall into that category, no question.

These forest roads, quiet and straight, are the fast lanes of migration. Sometime in the mid-1990s there were thought to be 400,000 Liberians living in Côte d'Ivoire. Some of them, from the more northern counties of Nimba and Grand Gedeh, passed into the Ivorian regions around Danané and Guiglo. But thousands and thousands of them passed through here, because Nero Village sits on the banks of the Cavally river and Liberia is on the other side. In the dry season you could swim to Liberia, crocodiles willing. In any season you could stand on this side of the bank and just about recognize someone standing on the other. Last July the headman of Prollo, another crossing point further upriver, said, 'Every day, the warriors on the Ivorian side and rebels of MODEL on the other glare at each other like fighting dogs.' The river crossing takes five minutes and, for most of the 1,000 or so Liberians living in Nero, it is an impossible trip.

The river cuts through the same kind of people. Grebo on this side, Grebo and Bassa on the other. They are related tribally and linguistically, so there has been lots of traffic back and forth, historically. Liberians have been coming here, on and off, whenever there has been a crisis. In other words, in 1989, 1990, 1991, 1992, 1993, 1994, 1995, 1996, 1997, 1998, 1999, 2000, 2001, 2002 and 2003. Ivorians went the other way, when war broke out in their country in 2002. But Nero only really became Refugee Central on 18 May 2003. Everyone here remembers the date, and that it was a Sunday, and that on that Sunday afternoon, the Ivorian-backed Liberian rebel force MODEL arrived in the Liberian town of Plibo. It arrived noisily. Heavy weapons, the ground shaking, the *tra-la-la* of AKs in the air. Over the next three days, about 6,000 people had crossed the Cavally, and were stuck in Nero Village. They couldn't go any further, because the village chief was worried that they were Liberians, and don't Liberians always bring war with them? Maybe they were rebels. So the refugees slept on the football field, on the river bank, on the ground of the village. The lucky ones were invited into the houses of friends or relatives. But most were not. They were so many, it was hard to walk without stepping on a person. They lived like this for three days, in the rainy season. Solid, driving rain. Three days, until Tabou's local governor — a good man, by all accounts — drove through the roads that were now rivers, and persuaded the chief to let the refugees in.

One thousand and seventy people stayed in Nero Village. A few hundred went to neighbouring villages like Gozon or Nero Cité, which are bigger and have bus stations (a bench outside a shack). They rented rooms or begged for shelter. They asked for food and were given it. But when they tried to go to Tabou, eighteen miles away, they were stopped. At the checkpoint outside Tabou, the locals would not let Liberians in. They had heard that Liberian rebels were involved in the fighting up in Nicla and Guiglou, further north in Côte d'Ivoire. They were sure that refugees had been recruited. The same people we gave refuge to! They come back and fight us! There was indignation, fury, and barely contained violence. And the refugees waited. They couldn't go back, because that was Liberia and MODEL. They couldn't go forward.

The locals were justified in their fury. Liberians had certainly come across the border and attacked Côte d'Ivoire. Liberian mercenaries — paid for in looting, as usual — were fighting on both sides of Côte d'Ivoire's war. The Ivorians had good reason to be suspicious. But it is illegal for a country to block its borders to refugees, according to the 1951 UN refugee convention. Even so, some countries do this blatantly, as the foul behaviour of Macedonia's border guards demonstrated in 1999, when they blocked the entry of Kosovar refugees, and wore rubber gloves and face masks to do it, as if being a refugee is catching. But for Côte d'Ivoire, this hostility was new.

In the past, such behaviour would have been rare in Africa. Africa specialists call the years between 1960 and 1980 the golden age of asylum, for the millions of refugees that African countries took in from their neighbours. It was generosity that far outstripped that of any western country. (In the early eighties the UK was receiving only 4,000 asylum-seekers a year.) But those were the golden years of Africa's economy, too, when newly independent countries were riding high. After it gained independence from France in 1960, Côte d'Ivoire's economy was excellent. Thanks partly to the use of imported labourers from Burkina Faso and Mali, Côte d'Ivoire became the world's largest cocoa producer and one of the top coffee producers. Its leader, Felix Houphouët-Boigny, ruled unchallenged until his death in 1993. With its stable economy, and a stable – if increasingly authoritarian – leadership, Côte d'Ivoire's treatment of its troubled Liberian visitors (until the mid-1990s) was exemplary. When 70,000 arrived in 1990 (or, more than the total number of asylum applications to the UK in 2003), Houphouët-Boigny called them 'our brothers in distress'. He set up an official refugee assistance zone (Zone d'Accueil des Réfugiés, or ZAR) in the western region, where refugees were free to settle and move around. He preached local integration and tolerance. He discouraged the setting up of camps but encouraged local villagers to make Liberians welcome. Even when they numbered 297,000 by the end of 1990, he let them stay.

By the mid-1990s the nation's economic success – it had been known as the Ivorian miracle – was petering out. Côte d'Ivoire was the world's biggest cocoa producer, but the market was weakening. GDP fell and kept falling. Tight resources mean tight belts and tight loyalties: Ivorian politicians, like politicians everywhere, discovered that there was mileage in blaming 'the foreigner' for whatever was expedient. Boigny's slogan had been 'the land for those who use it'; his successor and friend, Henri Konan-Bedié, preferred 'the land for its original owners'. Non-owners could be defined at will. As Bedié's closest political rival was from the north, northerners suddenly became less Ivorian, more foreign. The concept of 'Ivoirité', closely related to 'Aryan' on a moral scale, entered everyday conversation. Northerners now had trouble at checkpoints. They were harassed for having Muslim names.

It was vile politics. Some 'foreigners' were descended from Burkinabé families who had migrated fifty years before. They were suddenly foreign rather than useful. Ivoirité became the national public obsession, and foreigners the national bait. They were blamed for the crimes that any British tabloid reader would find familiar. Foreigners steal our land. They sponge off our economy. They raise house prices. As long as Houphouët-Boigny had ruled, as he did for thirty years, this was kept in check. When he died in 1993, xenophobia became permissible and profitable. It got votes by denying them to 'foreigners'.

Half a million people left Côte d'Ivoire, though they'd been there for generations. There was enough unrest and fury for safe, wealthy Côte d'Ivoire to turn into the African stereotype that it had always resisted. A bloodless coup happened in 1999. Elections in 2001 were abandoned when the coup leader General Robert Guei noticed he was losing. Disgruntled army officers exiled to Burkina Faso formed the MPCI (Mouvement Patriotique de la Côte d'Ivoire), and started a rebellion. On 19 September 2002 they simultaneously attacked the cities of Abidjan, Bouaké and Korhogo. For seven months afterwards, Abidjan was hell. (I drive across a bridge in Abidjan – apparently a functional, commercial city – with Bakayoko, the IRC driver, and he says, 'There were dead bodies all over this bridge. People jumped in and tried to swim. But they couldn't swim.')

In November two more rebel groups materialized, suspiciously close to the Liberian border. The Ivorian MJP (Movement for Justice and Peace) and MPIGO (Popular Movement for the Great West) were backed by Charles Taylor. So many movements. For accuracy, there should be a Movement for the Movement of People, as that's what they do best.

Ivorian president Laurent Gbagbo responded by recruiting anti-Taylor Liberians to fight alongside the army. Like rebels all over the world, he could cherry-pick, because they were all sitting behind a fence in a refugee camp in Nicla. He was also funding the Liberian rebel group MODEL.

Even the BBC's West Africa correspondent describes Côte d'Ivoire's war as 'very confusing'. I would prefer not to have to understand the Ivorian wars, because Liberia's are twisted enough. But wars in West Africa these days come in bulk. You can't have one without another. That's due in large part to the deliberate meddling of Charles Taylor, who supported the RUF in Sierra Leone, and the MJP and MPIGO in Côte d'Ivoire. But not only that: the Ivorian government sheltered and supported the anti-Taylor faction MODEL. Guinea's president sponsored LURD. Côte d'Ivoire's biggest rebel movement MPCI was fed, housed and encouraged by the state in Burkina Faso. Rebels don't usually have much respect for sovereign states, but in West Africa they didn't even notice the difference between them.

It's simpler for a refugee. Military analysts call the wars in the sub-region 'irregular conflicts'. But in a way they are quite regular. One Liberian refugee summed it up: 'Anyone with a gun is my enemy. Anyone!'

By early January the rebels had got close to Tabou. The

French military's Operation Licorne – 1,000 or so troops initially sent in to protect Côte d'Ivoire's 20,000 French citizens – was busy on the front line up north. Pushing back the rebels in the west was down to local militia formed from the Gueré tribespeople. The refugees were now in a whirlpool of war. There was MODEL on the Liberian side, and rebels here, too. They were in danger even in their place of safety. By 2002 the UN had designated the ZAR security phase IV. This is the second-highest notch' on the UN's ranking of danger, and it applied to the whole of Côte d'Ivoire's western region, from San Pedro on the coast to Guiglo in the north. In this area, one in six people is a refugee.

The other five in six are angry. Liberians from the Ivorian refugee camps, and from MODEL, were known, in the words of Human Rights Watch, to have 'participated in dozens of killings, rapes, and other acts of violence against civilians in and around Toulepleu, Bangolo and Blolékin. At least sixty civilians were killed in the worst single incident documented in Bangolo in March 2003.' The locals saw this, understandably, as ingratitude. And they chose to target all Liberians, for the crimes of a few.

'Last January and February [2003] were the worst times,' says the brisk and efficient UNHCR field officer in Tabou. 'They were going home at night and not knowing who was coming for them. It was pure terror.' A thousand refugees moved into the UNHCR office compound. The compound is not large; only three or four 4WD vehicles can fit in its yard. It must have been hell. But they had no choice; even if they'd wanted to go back to Liberia, the locals wouldn't let them. Nevertheless, the UNHCR began organizing repatriation. Liberians were transported by minibus to Prollo, where they were due to be sent across by motor boats, rented in Tabou and sent along the Atlantic then upriver to Prollo. But one day the boats didn't turn up. Local chiefs had decided the river was cursed. It wasn't safe for boats. They were persuaded to rent out five canoes, but the river was flowing strongly, and the canoes rocked too much. The locals didn't want the refugees around, because they were probably rebels, but they didn't want them to leave either, in case they were going for reinforcements.

They blocked checkpoints and made threats. They chose not to make a difference between aggressive rebels and vulnerable, scared people. It was, said a UNHCR emergency coordinator at the time, 'very sad. The opposition of the local people is just enormous.'

'It was hell,' says the field officer who had 1,000 refugees camped in her front yard. 'But the thing about Liberians is, they never asked me for blankets or food. All they asked for was a durable solution.'

This sounds like jargon talking. (The same officer referred constantly to people as 'caseloads', which is what people have to become in humanitarian language.) But it may be true. In the classroom in Nero Village, every refugee knows the words 'durable solution'. They might know that most of the world's refugees are still waiting for one, because it is a harder thing to provide than tarpaulin and T-shirts. They know that the three accepted durable solutions, in descending order of desirability, are Repatriation in the home country, Local Integration in a second country or Resettlement in a third country. They know which they want, too: the one that is the safest. 'We want to go home,' they say, but not till the guns have stopped. Not till they've gathered all the guns hidden in the bushes, in concrete-lined pits, the weapons coated in oil for protection against the elements. Until the guns in the bushes are made safe, they'd prefer resettlement.

'I went home!' says one young man, angrily. 'They offered

us repatriation in 2000 and I took it. We'd had elections, I thought the conditions were a little bit all right.' He came back in May 2003, followed by the sound of rocket launchers. He says, 'I can't live by rumour. I waited to see if the rebels came. When I heard BOOM BOOM, I ran. It's better to stay on this side, even with the problems.' He shrugs. 'What's the use?'

Local integration is the least favoured option for this classroom. 'It's not safe here,' they say. 'It's not safe there, and it's not safe here.' Even the UNHCR representative has defined Liberians' situation in Côte d'Ivoire as being between a rock and a hard place. The UNHCR regional representative told the *Washington Post* that the situation facing displaced refugees – because now they were both – 'is not even human misery. It's worse than that.'

Back at the time of the big crossings, in May and June, the Gueré warriors set up a checkpoint at Tabou. It's still there – a couple of oil drums and some shrubs in the road – and back then, it served to hold back thousands of Liberians. UNHCR stepped in. There was persuasion and negotiation. There was probably, from the refugees, much begging for forgiveness. I didn't understand this, the first time I heard it. 'I couldn't get through the checkpoint,' they will say, 'so I begged for forgiveness.' They mean compassion or mercy. But they say 'forgiveness', as if being a refugee is a sin. Either way, there was an agreement: a transit centre would be set up in a cassava field near the checkpoint. Not too near to Tabou, but not too far either. A transit centre, because this is less formal than a refugee camp, and supposed to be temporary. It helped calm tempers. Zinc booths were erected on sandy ground to house 700 refugees. In two months, 30,000 refugees had come to Tabou, and 4,000 were staying in the transit centre. The rest were making do, somewhere.

But the refugees in Nero Village didn't get to the transit centre in the beginning, when the trucks were laid on, and now they can't. It's a fine day when I visit, and the river looks fresh, and the forest is green. It's a nicer place than the transit centre, which seethes with heat and boredom. But actually, Nero Village is just a very pretty prison.

The Ivorian IRC workers are sympathetic to refugees, by default and by inclination. They must have hung around them a lot, because I'm surprised, after hearing them all speak French constantly, to see them stand up in the workshop and speak fluent Liberian English. Right down to the 'o'. UNHCR-o! Repatriation-o!

They're a nice bunch, even if Marthe, the IRC staffer sitting in the back during the ride into Nero, launches into 'If you're happy and you know it, clap your hands.' It's even worse in French.

Simon-Pierre is one of eight field agents for IRC's Gender-Based Violence programme. Most of them seem to have come for this workshop, and they take the teaching in turns. Simon-Pierre's sympathy for refugees almost turned him into one. In January 2003, when hostility to Liberians was at its height, word reached him that his support of Liberians was not popular in Tabou, where such support was at that moment thin on the ground. Simon-Pierre was threatened to his face, and thought it wise to leave, at 5 o'clock one morning, for Abidjan. He didn't return for months. Later he took a short trip into Liberia. I ask why, trying as usual to calculate which rebels were doing what in Liberia at that time, but knowing that some of them were certainly doing something. 'I was doing a favour to a friend in America. He'd lost touch with his mother and asked me to go and find her.' He looked for her first among the crowds in Nero Village, then he crossed. He was probably the only person going that way, because it was madness to do it. He looks under-whelmed. 'It wasn't easy,' he says. 'But I found her.'

This is a dream class for a teacher: 25 eager pupils, notebooks ready, desperate to use their brains and fill the tedium. The Lutheran church is one of two in the village: the other is known as the 'refugee church'. 'What faith does that follow?' I ask. 'None, specially. It's just where the refugees go.'

The IRC runs workshops every month or so, on a variety of subjects: gender-based violence, child protection and edu-cation. There's a GBV field agent on hand in the village almost every day, just to be there, and to organize small projects for the women, such as baking and soap-making. That's more than it sounds, when there's nothing to do. This workshop is the first of its kind, though, because the staff had special training from an IRC employee flown in from New York. She couldn't speak French and they couldn't understand her English, but some things must have got through. Most noticeably, the skill of dealing with the class's awkward questions. 'Let's put that in the waiting room,' says Simon-Pierre. 'That's one for the wait-ing room,' says Sondé-Pierre, a protection officer.

The use of the waiting room is a sign the training worked. That's fine, except the waiting room is never visited again, and I'd like an answer to the class's awkward questions too. For example: 'Local integration? So why the Ivorians say now they don't want to see no Liberians in the bush cutting wood?'

Or: 'Freedom of movement? But we have to pay 1,000 CFA [Communauté financière africaine, the Ivorian currency] at every checkpoint. So if you haven't got an ID card and you have to move around and you can't – do you still have that basic right?'

One of the class gets annoyed. He's obviously been to work-shops before – I see him consulting notes from October 2003 –

but now he's had enough. 'I have never been to Tabou up to this time, because I can't go! I stay in this place. I can't travel, I can't go anywhere. UNHCR come, you come and it's talk, talk, talk, and the end is zero.' The reason for the checkpoints, I'm told later, is that the prefect of Tabou is aware of the problem, but what can he do? The soldiers who man the checkpoints are poorly paid. The money they get from charging refugees makes their poor pay tolerable. Enough not to mutiny, or join the rebels, or give the prefecture any kind of headache. The prefect is powerless.

But Simon-Pierre can't say this, so he puts this point in the waiting room. It's not his fault: there is nothing he can say to mollify, because there is nothing to be done. Bertrand, a jovial field officer who's sitting next to me on the cramped wooden bench, leans over and whispers to the irate man. 'We're very sorry about that. We've got to talk to the police about it, but it's very hard.'

'But I've been running since 1990!'

'I know,' says Bertrand. 'I know.'

I can't tell who's Liberian and who's Ivorian in the village. There's no outward sign, no ID bracelet. A refugee doesn't have any distinguishing features. The clothes might be shabbier – the refugee chairman says he owns only one T-shirt – and they might be thinner (he says he has one meal a day if he's lucky). But otherwise, there's no sign. So I say, 'Bonjourhello' to everyone, and the answer is usually 'Yeah, goo'mornin'.' There are four Liberians to every Ivorian here. In some other villages, like Georgetown, it's ten to one. The asylum-seeking population of the UK was 0.008 per cent of the population last year. Even the biggest ethnic minority is only 3.5 per cent. I form a plan to send *Daily Mail* journalists to Georgetown for sensitivity training, with a copy of some of their headlines

– 'asylum-seekers overrunning Britain/the NHS/the housing market' – a calculator and a British census.

I walk through the village to the river's edge with Simon-Pierre. It takes five minutes. We pass a small boy crying in the street. He is scooped up by a passing parent and introduced as Namo, which means 'don't go back' in Grebo. It's a very appropriate refugee name, I say hopefully, but Simon-Pierre is unconvinced. 'They probably had some children die in the family, so it just means they don't want him to go to heaven yet.' Ask a Liberian how big their family is, and they will unfailingly tell you the number of 'livingchildren', as if it's one word. They know better than to presume they'll survive.

At the river a man is pushing off a pirogue filled with people. When I want to take his picture, he shouts up, 'Don't take my picture! I'm a rebel. I'm with MODEL. Don't take my picture.' I think he's joking at first, but the look on Simon-Pierre's face tells me he's not.

The crossing takes a few minutes. At the time of the biggest refugee movements, those few minutes must have seemed endless, because they were accompanied by the sound of rocket launchers, clear as anything on the Liberian side. Even so, the pirogues worked from 7 a.m. to 7 p.m. straight. They charged 500 CFA per person, took twenty-two people per crossing, and sometimes let wounded people go free.

On the bank, young men are loafing with Ali-G caps and no apparent reason to be there. Beneath them there are rusting machinery parts. Simon-Pierre says they were brought across by looters, and sooner or later they'll be removed and sold. This used to be the looters' favourite crossing point, until a border post and two bored policemen were installed. Every motorbike you see in the Tabou region was probably stolen from Liberia. Fighters took copper wire, insulation materials, everything. In Liberia and Sierra Leone, people said the fighters were on

Operation Pay Yourself, because it was lootable and movable. After the policemen arrived, the looting route just shifted to a point further upriver, where there's no border post. The rebels still cross, but just to do their shopping. Salt is cheaper on this side, and there's a video club.

Under a shelter in the village, a group of refugees have gathered to talk. They've all been here since last year. They weren't expecting their possessions to follow them. One said, 'The rebels come over here all the time. I saw them selling my property. I saw my icebox, my solar panels, some other things. With my name on!' There were eight of them; they weren't armed – the police don't let arms through, or they haven't yet – but they were dangerous. 'They said I was spoiling business,' he continued. 'People around learned that the things were mine, so they were refusing to buy them. They told me to come back to Liberia with them to show them where I had left my things. I refused, of course. They said, go back to Liberia, you'll have problems.'

None of these men has been back to Liberia, and they all refuse to go. They say they're not military men, so they would suffer at the hands of people who are. They say they have already suffered enough. When they say 'sufferin'' they sound like they have just stepped off a South Carolina plantation. You can hear the slave talking, and the word is as weighty for them as it was for any slave.

The men are telling their stories one by one. One man leaves, but he comes back and waits patiently for his turn. His name is Augustin Weah, and he was a tax inspector. That means he worked for the government, and that means he was a target. He disappeared to take his medication, because he's had high blood pressure since he saw his sister dismembered in front of him. 'She was forty. They cut her to pieces, and then they told me to bury her.' They were Liberia Peace Council, a faction opposed to Taylor, and the date was Sunday, 10 October 1992. 'They said that I was pro-Taylor because I was a tax collector. They took me somewhere else, and a school friend who was with the rebels freed me.' Some years later he resumed his job, and the war came again. Different rebels, same result. 'This was May 2003. I'd been assigned to Plibo. We heard from the BBC they closed the road between Plibo and Zwedru. The women and children had run, but the men had stayed because they can run better than small children. They arrested me again, for the same reason.' I say, how did the rebels know you were the tax collector? They weren't local. He says what several non-Liberians have said to me. 'Liberians can point fingers at their friends.' He says this as a fact, nothing more. He is anxious to tell his story properly, and his hands are shaking. 'If you had a BP instrument,' he says, 'you would see my pressure is high.' This time he was arrested with his brother Samuel. There wasn't time for them to cut up Samuel because MODEL attacked, and in the confusion they escaped. But Samuel took a bullet and died, and Augustin took the decision never to go back to Liberia if he could help it.

He says it's difficult for him to get food. UNHCR and WFP gave some rations out in the beginning, but they haven't distributed anything for months. He eats by begging or good fortune. It is difficult for all the refugees to get food, since the Ivorians stopped being generous with their land. They still let them pick breadfruit, but not cassava. Not palm nuts. Not anything much. 'Breadfruit is refugee food. It's the only food we can find.' There is fish in the river, surely? Augustin almost shivers. His hands shake on the table. 'It's too close to Liberia. I won't go there.'

But Nero Village is close to Liberia, I say. If I turned and walked, I could be at the river bank in a hundred paces. It is UNHCR policy to place refugee populations away from borders. Borders are too close to trouble. They leave refugees open to harassment and recruitment. Here we're as close as you can get. Why haven't they moved? 'But we can't go to Tabou. We need logistics. Where is the money? You go to the gates and you pay. You show the refugee ID, and they tear it up. If you go to a checkpoint, just take note — if you see some blacks sitting, go and ask them. They will tell you, "They catch me." What for? "Documents." You will see who are refugees, because they'll be the detained ones. So we are not able to go, even if we want to.'

Rock and hard place. 'Some people don't believe we're at risk. But we see the rebels come over here with their liquor and they say, "We can easily come and get you." When you are hearing this, do you think you feel free to go back?' They often hear gunshots, still. They tell me to come back anytime. Anytime in the future. They'll still be here.

In the workshop the class has moved on to refugee rights. On the blackboard Simon-Pierre has drawn — very badly — two stick figures. This is Koné, this is John. Koné is Ivorian, John is Liberian. Both have left their homes, but one is an IDP and one is a refugee. Everyone is taking notes, but I get the impression it's just for something to do. They know the difference between being an IDP and a refugee, because they have seesawed between both conditions for years. Even when Grace translates Simon-Pierre's English into Grebo, for the *mamies* ('grannies') who are attending, I hear the English terms — IDP, refugee, displaced — among the Grebo. Such words crossed languages a long time ago. They are all that people think about.

A young man called Alfred is paying attention with fierce concentration. He is a tough audience, one of those people who always have their hands up. He'd annoy most teachers. But when he answers the question about the differences between an

IDP's and a refugee's rights, his phrasing is far superior to anything on the blackboard. 'John has privileges, but Koné has rights. A privilege is when you get for example free food. Rights are what you have access to. Privileges are when you don't have rights but someone can give it to you anytime.'

And they can withdraw them anytime. Alfred hasn't finished. 'For example, you are living in the town here and you are a refugee, you are not a citizen. The town people have their bush, but when it comes to share the bush, they may not give you some. But you all have rights to go to the waterside and draw water and drink. Everybody got the right to live. In the whole world, as you long as you're coming with no arms, you got the right to live.'

This is fine talk. But refugee conventions are one thing; persuading a villager to let you chop wood is another. The difficult relationship between the 'international community' and the host country can be simplified into one real example: there was a situation in Tanzania when UNHCR distributed tarpaulin for tents for Rwandan refugees, but they didn't distribute wood for their construction. The sticks had to come from the bush, and the refugees had to collect it. A UNHCR paper describes the consequences: 'A free-for-all attitude is created within the refugee communities with regard to firewood, poles, timber, grass, animal fodder and any other plant material available within walking distance.' Relations were understandably strained between refugee and host.

To be fair, Ivorians have hosted refugees for years, in numbers that would terrify any western politician, and they receive little financial support from the internationals. Western countries would have stopped refugees going into the bush years earlier, especially if you substitute 'benefits system' for 'wood-gathering'. Either way, there's a dead end, with a long queue of refugees leading up to it.

These days, there are reports of Liberians being refused work on the plantations, because they don't have ID cards. Other reports claim they are being beaten up or flogged. An aid worker says to me, 'I won't say anything against the Ivorians here, because that would endanger the refugees. And I don't want that to happen.' But one refugee says, 'It's difficult to travel round here, because you can go missing in action.' When I invite him to say more, he asks to change the subject, and suddenly drains a glass of water, too rapidly for comfort.

A thunderstorm starts after the lunch break. It is violent rain, and after ten minutes the red dusty ground is flooded and the classroom roof starts to leak. Refugees insist on swapping seats with me, anxious to protect my minidisc, but I go instead to find some young women refugees. I've heard things about sexual harassment and prostitution of unaccompanied women. But most of them are out gathering wood or food; they start straggling in later, drenched and empty-handed. The only one home, apparently, is Mary Weah.

She lives on the far side of the village. The road through it is now a line of several deep pools. Children with bigger bellies than they should have – malnutrition is at 4 per cent in these areas, they tell me at the IRC, but it could easily explode – play in the mud and water, while I calculate how many waterborne diseases and conditions I can think of. Cholera. Diarrhoea. Dysentery. In Mary's dark, dank hut the seats are two pieces of wood, and her children are naked. Chickens peck in the corner, safe from the water that has risen to near the entrance. After ten minutes the hut is nearly flooded. The rainy season lasts months. In the rainy season the roads through the forest become creeks. The village gets stuck between water and water, and no NGOs can get through.

Mary is illiterate, young and shy. She lost her husband –

literally – on the way from Robertsburg, in Maryland county, over the river. She paid $100 Liberian to cross with her three children, but now she has only two. 'Things were really bad. We had no money, no food.' In December her thirteen-year-old son Prince begged her to let him go to Liberia to look for food. She refused for two days, but then she said yes. 'I was expecting him back in December but he's not back. I don't have the money to go and look for him. He didn't carry nothing, he just followed the road. It's taking him a long time now.'

Mary doesn't understand my English, so I ask Simon-Pierre the questions in French – his native language – and he translates them into his English. He's the only IRC worker with a French accent and without a Liberian one, but Mary still understands him better. I want to know if Mary has problems because she's alone, without a husband. She is unprotected. Simon-Pierre translates her reply as something to do with gathering wood in the forest. But that wasn't the question! 'I know,' he says, in French, which Mary doesn't speak. 'Sometimes when women say nothing, that means yes.'

Not many women speak during the workshop. It's difficult to butt in, with all the men talking. But after two and a half hours of the workshop, lunch is served. It's Liberian food – very spicy, and with unidentifiable meat – and I don't eat much. The refugees eat it like hungry people, quickly and savouringly. Afterwards, some women ask to speak to me. I'd noticed Musu Russell in the workshop, because she was one of the few women who spoke up, and she didn't have a Liberian accent. She's from Sierra Leone, and her husband is Liberian. He used to work for MSF in Liberia, earning 75,000 CFA a month; she was an elementary school teacher and earned enough. Now she teaches in the 'non-formal education' classes run by IRC in the village, but her children are too old for them. 'I'm worried they'll slip through my fingers. There are refugees who send their children out to work in the wee-wee hours, to earn 1,000 CFA. It's terrible.'

In the nearby village of Gozon there is a bistro that opens from 6 p.m. to 6 a.m., Friday nights only. On Friday nights workers from the plantations come, as do the Ivorian soldiers who are stationed nearby. It is an epicentre of income, in a village of impoverished refugees. No one should have been surprised when young Liberian girls, alone and separated from their families, built themselves shacks around the bistro. It's better money than gathering charcoal. Refugees in Tabou tell me that other refugees send their girls out to 'walk up and down', for the same purpose.

Musu has a lovely manner and a lilt in her accent. When she says she built six houses over the years, it sounds pretty. 'Let me see. I built one house in Gozon. I built two in Liberia, then two here, then I built two again in the last war.' She doesn't bother putting glass in the windows any more, because it gets broken. Plastic windows, mud walls, sticks and stones. 'Yes,' says another woman nearby, 'they're refugee houses. Not ones we'll stay in.'

Later, when I'm back in London, Musu writes me a letter. She says Africa needs a lot of help. 'It needs to be mended in a wonderful way,' and she hopes that the techniques of white people can do it. She writes that she wants help to get on the US resettlement programme that is under way in Côte d'Ivoire. 'The reason I have is that I'm tired with running away, children holding guns and looting, all your belongings that you work for for a long time will vanish that one day, your school, house, and children.' She puts her address as Refugees Camp, Nero Village, Ivory Coast.

I take this as a permanent address. So what, if there are

conventions about free movement, basic human rights. So what, if there is theory on the blackboard. Even star refugee pupil Alfred doesn't put much faith in it, not really. 'I just do this workshop to settle my mind. It takes my mind off what I saw in Liberia – dead bodies, people killed. It helps.' He knows the theories of refugee policy, but he knows the practice better. He says, unassailably, 'This is our experience. Another man has a citizen's rights but we have a refugee identity. As a refugee, you can't go very far.'

# 7. New Jersey City

'Refugees don't cause problems. They already have problems.'

(UNHCR tolerance campaign, Côte d'Ivoire, 2003)

The road to Tabou is six long boring hours of red dust and fatal potholes. The road is long and straight, stretching all the way from Abidjan. 'Potholes' doesn't do the craters justice: these are holes that literally stop a 4WD in its tracks.

There is a plane that flies between Abidjan and Tabou, but IRC usually sends its staff back and forth by road. Two drivers are sent forth from either end to meet halfway. They exchange passengers, and return to their office. This is the theory, anyway, but IRC established its Côte d'Ivoire office only in mid-2003, and things aren't quite sorted, logistically. There are no radios in the cars, neither the squawking walkie-talkie that's the standard aid-worker accessory, nor the music-playing version. The cars are new and supplied by UNHCR, and there hasn't been time to fit them properly yet.

There's not a lot to do in the car, nor in the extra three hours we spend at Sassandra, waiting for the other vehicle to come. I spend some time calculating the weight that women are carrying, but I underestimate them and their weight. Later, a frail-looking young woman refugee tells me she carries 50 kg of charcoal on her head, daily.

I have time to work out the Ivorian highway code: if you want to overtake, the driver in front indicates towards the nearside of the road if it's not safe, and towards the offside if it is. But interpretation of safety must vary, after the second driver in a row invites my driver to overtake on a blind hill. Safety is a constant preoccupation on this road; I mentally breathe in when we pass rickety buses lurching through potholes like listing ships and inspiring as little confidence. Later, IRC's Tabou field coordinator Jennifer told me that one day she saw one topple over onto a nun who was overtaking. Then she watched as the nun died slowly, trapped in her car.

There is a sort of entertainment to be had in collecting checkpoint styles. There are too many to count, on the 400 or so kilometres between Abidjan and Tabou. It doesn't feel like it here, but Côte d'Ivoire is at war, and checkpoints are necessary. They are barbed wire or oil drums, shrubs and concrete. Some of them have a small boy who glumly withdraws a lethal-looking strip of spiked metal, when he spots the magic IRC sticker that is an unspoken laissez-passer.

Locals get stopped; internationals usually don't, not in these parts. It's not the same in rebel-held territory up north; the IRC programme officer in Man, a genial Frenchman called Christian, doesn't bother wearing a watch any more because he got sick of replacing the ones that the rebels took off him. He always sets off early, too, because sensible people realize that rebels are drunk by afternoon, and checkpoints get tougher.

I get a glimpse of this different reality only once, when there are no white man's 4WDs available, and I have to travel by taxi from Tabou to San Pedro. The taxi takes an hour to arrive, because there are only two in town with the right papers to get through checkpoints. IRC stickers are put on the taxi, but the car still isn't aid-world white, even if I am. So every checkpoint and every soldier produces the same scene. A slow reading out loud of the official letter, finger underlining the words. A pause for no reason. Another pause to underline the lack of reason of the pause. Then that little waggle of the fingers that means things that diplomats have spent years trying to enshrine in documents: freedom of movement, human rights, dignity. All that, in one waggle.

Amadou Koné is driving me during the second leg to Tabou. His car has no radio, either, so he is fond of singing a dreadful Ivorian reggae song about Nagasaki. A song of destruction is fitting accompaniment to the road, which is getting worse. There are craters that appear to be designed, they are so deep and permanent. 'Ha!' says Koné. 'This road is ten years old! We paid taxes for it!' He laughs at the absurdity, and says it might be fixed this year, because elections are coming. We drive through San Pedro, which Koné calls 'San Pedro, *sans pitié*' (San Pedro the pitiless). It's his home town, and even he isn't used to how much of a dump it is. Dust, engine fumes, foulness. This is the second biggest port in Côte d'Ivoire, and it should be rich. It probably is rich, but the money has long since levitated beyond pothole level, where it should have at least paused.

San Pedro is famous for two things. There's an expat surfing scene here, which you can find out about through a surf shop in Abidjan. And it was at this port, in 1996, that the ship *Bulk Challenge* was refused entry. The ship was carrying Liberian refugees. No one's sure how many, but it was over a thousand, on a ship with a passenger-carrying capacity of about a hundred. The refugees had left Monrovia on 5 May that year, because on 6 April fighting began that was so terrible, young children who weren't even born then know that date.

Liberia's provisional authorities tried in vain to arrest faction leader Roosevelt Johnson; 3,000 people were killed, 300,000 became displaced. You'd think that both these figures are good enough reasons to get on a ship and get as far away as possible. But the Ivorians didn't see a ship full of refugees. They were sick of Liberians and their wars, particularly as there was trouble brewing in their own country too. After San Pedro had turned away the ship, the Interior Minister said, 'There are 2,065 people on the boat who are rebels.' The ship tried to dock in Ghana and was sent to Nigeria. Ghana only agreed to take it in when it developed mechanical trouble, and because the western media were actually paying attention. A later search of the ship revealed no weapons.

Liberians are Africa's pariahs now. When the Liberian refugee camp near Guiglo was attacked in 2003, UNHCR tried desperately to get another African country to take the refugees. Every country they approached refused. But, for once, the US came to the rescue.

On the other side of San Pedro a large convoy of white vehicles zooms past. I count six buses, a few 4WDs, some flashing lights. The buses are labelled GTZ, the logo of the German state development agency, and they're taking lucky Liberians to Abidjan, because they've been provisionally accepted on the US resettlement programme. Earlier, a smaller convoy of buses, less flashy, and fewer in number, had gone past transporting Burkinabé Ivorians. Migrants who had lived here for years, who decided that their best option was to go to a country they had never lived in, but that Ivorians had decided was their home.

I hadn't known about the US resettlement programme before I arrived in Tabou. I'd wanted to write about a new UK programme that was supposed to start in Ghana, but the Home Office was striving to be as unhelpful as it could – 'it's not the right time to talk about it' – and the programme kept getting postponed. Anyway, the UK resettlement is for only 500 Liberians – hardly significant, against the 6,000 people that the US is planning to take in.

The resettlement programme is causing tension. On Sunday

morning we drive to Tabou's transit centre. The UNHCR programme officer is visiting at the same time, and she is hot and harried. She says, 'Don't mention resettlement here, on any account. Only fifty people out of the four thousand camp residents are eligible and there's a lot of anger.' Jennifer says not to worry about it. 'They'll think that any white person here has to be involved in resettlement. You wouldn't be here otherwise.'

You don't have to mention the word, though, to see where people's aspirations lie. The zinc booths – actually, hangars – are supplemented by huge green tarpaulin tents, and people write their dreams on the outside of both. Booth 3A has become New Jersey City. Here is the State of Illinois. There is Chicago and Los Angeles. Over there, puzzlingly, is the Union of Soviet Socialist Republics. 'Huh,' says Anthony. 'I wouldn't live there. It's probably even poorer than the rest.'

Anthony is the refugee chairman for Tabou. That's a considerable job. Tabou's population is 28,000 without the refugees, who in the whole Tabou region number four times that. So he has two assistants to help him, especially as he also works full-time as an education officer for the IRC. When she was still learning the ropes, Jennifer had met him one day in the camp, where IRC had made the mistaken gesture of giving out T-shirts. 'I know now,' Jennifer says, 'that if you give out one thing, you have to have four thousand of them.' But back then they didn't know that. The T-shirts were for women who completed a GBV workshop, but people just wanted the shirts, not the workshop. And they wanted them because they were T-shirts, not for anything that was written on them. A change of wardrobe is a precious thing in a refugee camp. But it's not unheard of.

'When I first saw a refugee camp,' says Julie, a young American nurse who runs the Action Contre La Faim therapeutic feeding centre, 'I was surprised to see commerce. I expected refugees to have nothing.'

In fact, there are little stalls here, selling peanuts and trinkets. There is a young man with a new bike, which he bought from the proceeds of his 'small small business'. Young Ivorian girls come in bearing small plastic bags of dubious 'mineral' water. You have to be careful, walking round the camp, not to step on fish laid out to dry, patches of dull silver things on the sandy ground. There are small gardens with sparse cassava leaves and other greens. Under a hangar a group of small boys hammer away at scrap metal, making toys for themselves. A truck, a bus, a 4WD like the NGOs have. There is activity here. Just not enough.

The industriousness of refugees is a subject of much academic discussion. The stereotype – a helpless refugee, dependent on hand-outs – is inaccurate. Buduburam camp in Ghana has the reputation for being the best camp for Liberian refugees in West Africa (Liberia has been spitting out refugees long enough for someone to draw up a Top Ten). It's also a case study.

When 40,000 refugees arrived in 1990, UNHCR did what it usually does, laudably; it set up a camp, 35 kilometres from Accra, and distributed food, non-food items (blankets, tents, some pots and pans) and provided classes in skills such as tie-dyeing and carpentry. In 1997, after Charles Taylor won the elections, 3,000 refugees agreed to return to Liberia. UNHCR cut off distribution to the remaining 40,000, deciding that Liberia was safe enough (wrong), and that deprivation would encourage refugees to go home voluntarily (also wrong). At this point, the many people who believe that refugees live off and live for hand-outs expected disaster. Instead, refugees turned entrepreneurs. They used small loans and money from relatives abroad, and the camp kept going. It kept going so well, it became the subject of an Oxford University study into how refugees live without humanitarian assistance.

Today, 45,000 refugees still live in Buduburam. There is a market, shops and several phone companies. (The first 'communication centre', BuduCom, was set up in 1995 by a man on a bike with a mobile phone. Your correspondent calls his phone; he gets on his bike and brings it to you.) There are even a couple of internet cafés. It's almost a self-reliant town. The conclusion, wrote the Oxford University researcher, is that 'the crux of the matter seems to be that refugees will utilize whatever opportunities remain open to them in order to maximize their situation.'

This conclusion depends on the assumption that opportunities are available. Again and again, when I ask refugees why they can't work or travel or improve things, they say simply, 'But I am not Ivorian. How can I?'

The opportunities in Tabou transit centre are limited. But they are no more limited than opportunities outside. Agrippa Choloplay has lived in Côte d'Ivoire for fourteen years, since his father was killed along with Samuel Doe in 1990. He lives in the town of Tabou, but things are hard. 'We used to cut wood and sell it. We'd earn about 2,000 CFA daily. It was enough to buy food. Now, no way. They don't let us do that, since the crisis started.' He makes money by helping fishermen gather in the nets, when they let him. This is once or twice a week, so his family eats only once a day. In the transit centre, at least, there are three meals a day, even if they all involve bulgur wheat. For this reason, some of its registered residents don't live there, but they register for food aid.

There are complaints about the food, of course, and about the accommodation – the booths are noisy, and you have to sleep near strangers. But this is a transit centre, not a refugee camp, and it's subject to lower standards. Even so, there are dozens of latrines, seemingly clean and each bearing a bizarre hand-painted sign. The men's are decorated with pictures of a white man with a bushy Zapata moustache and hairdo. He looks like an extra on a seventies cop show. The picture on the women's is even odder: a buxom white lady, thrusting out her breasts, her hands on her hips. Perhaps this artistic flourish can be explained by the fact that a German charity built them.

There are several NGOs working in the camp, though fewer than at Wilson Corner IDP camp in Monrovia, which bears a sign that reads like an NGO shopping list. I count about fifteen acronyms, before the car drives on. In Tabou, Caritas runs the clinic and ACF the therapeutic feeding centre. All the malnourished babies in Tabou come here – the refugee ones, that is. It is a frustrating irony for aid workers that their mandate doesn't usually cover the host population. A sick Ivorian baby here would get more international assistance over the border in Liberia.

The babies are tiny and the booth is baking hot. Julie is the only international worker here, because she's waiting to train some local staff. For now, it's her and a handful of volunteers. One of them, Chris, jumped onto a ship one day in Monrovia without telling his family. 'It was there, so I got on it.' He got word to an uncle in Italy, who told his family in Monrovia that he wasn't dead.

I don't know much about ACF, but I like their business cards: a dotted line where the name should be, to be filled in as appropriate. 'Yeah, that sums them up,' said someone from IRC. 'They save money in good ways.' Humanitarian organizations have personalities. Caritas runs clinics, GTZ builds things. So does IRC, which is probably the largest NGO with a mandate in refugee assistance. (The UN is made of member states, so UNHCR is a governmental organization.) IRC says it provides developmental relief – not hand-outs, but help-ups.

Other agencies call it 'the construction company'. At the transit centre it undertakes WATSAN (water and sanitation), GBV and informal education programmes. They do further work in the refugee population outside the transit centre, because there are 4,000 refugees in the centre, which leaves 36,000 outside it. Some of their work includes emptying wells of human remains for Ivorians. In one area, after the war, only 5 per cent of wells were operational, because so many bodies had been tipped in them.

Tabou's residents outline their situation very simply: they are 'in the fence', and everyone and everything else – jobs, money, opportunity – is outside. IRC's education programmes officially have to be called 'informal', though they have the usual trappings of school – teachers, lessons, books. They can't be called schools, because the Ivorian government objects, understandably, to a parallel English-language system being set up. This was why, less understandably, UNHCR abruptly terminated English-language refugee schools in 1999, and has yet to replace them. Most refugees don't speak French, and it's hard to go to school when you don't speak the language. 'What, do you expect a fourteen-year-old to start in elementary class?' one asks. There is much indignation about the schooling situation, because these are poor countries, and education is power. There is concern about it, too, because bored teenagers with this much level of frustration sometimes grow up into rebels.

In the dusty football field at the transit centre, I see two young women, in their Sunday best, hugging each other. Joetta and Esther are teenagers and sisters, and bored. 'One minute I was doing my school exams in Harper,' says Esther, 'and the next minute MODEL arrives and I'm a refugee. It's not easy!' Of course it's boring here, they say. There's nothing to do. They play football, or do chores, or do their hair. All around the camp, there are little huddles of women, combing in weaves. But there are also more natural looks than there would be normally: palm grease is expensive and not everyone can afford it. 'I want to go back to Liberia,' says Esther. 'I don't,' says Joetta with a wicked smile. 'I'll come back to London with you. OK?'

Joetta and Esther are here to watch a circus. It is a circus with good intentions, but it's going badly wrong. UNHCR has recruited the Ivorian reggae group Magic System to come and play a concert. They played one a couple of days earlier in the village of Gozon, and the intention was to repeat it here. Magic System are one of two notable pop acts that are fronting UNHCR's tolerance campaign. Theme: 'Your tolerance can make the difference.' There are posters and T-shirts, all with sensible slogans. One of them reads, 'A refugee doesn't cause problems, he has problems.'

Magic System released a song for UNHCR, called 'SOS Refugié'. The UNHCR information officer in Abidjan gives me a copy, but I can't understand it and the song's terrible. But Magic's heart (there's only one man, really) is in the right place – he's flown from Paris just to do goodwill events, and he's already taken a tour of the transit centre and asked all the right questions. So say the UNHCR people, at least. Everyone else sees a mess. It's noon on Sunday, and the churches are in full singing voice in two booths right next to the stage where the performance is supposed to be. After a greeting ceremony by a young girl in skimpy cloth and chalked skin, who throws rice and gives him a kola nut, Magic looks stumped. He doesn't want to disturb the church services, but he can't stay because he has to get back to Abidjan. The result is a flop: the church services will last only another forty minutes, but the Magic System road show gets back in the 4WDs and leaves. It also leaves a mini-riot: there's a box of cassettes to be given out, but not four thousand of them. An orderly queue forms, and then there's trouble. Scuffles, near-fights, resentment.

I'm no camp expert, so I wonder if my expectations were too high. But Jennifer's not too impressed either. Afterwards, when I'm interviewing two refugee officials, they say, 'The churches did it deliberately. They'd promised to use some other booths – there are several empty ones, further from the stage – but some people were angry. They don't want a concert. They want rice, and resettlement.'

The two officials are middle-aged men. Tanneh-Bartee Senneh – Bartee for short – is Co-chairman of Administration of the Refugee Committee. Reverend Moses G. Hyneh is Co-chairman of Operations. They have laminated ID cards to prove it, though it's not clear what the committee does to require so many staff. I see Bartee early one morning, doing his rounds. 'We do it every day, just to check to see if there's been any violence or anything.' The camp has had problems with sexual violence. 'It's not UNHCR policy to provide partitions, so everyone in the booth has to sleep next to strangers. Before people could afford to set up partitions, there was no privacy. Women had nowhere to change. They had to come back and hold their lappas like this –' he mimes a woman who is changing under a cloth, like she's on a beach – 'and it was very embarrassing for them.' There are things you get used to, as a refugee, and things you never do, like being naked in public. No matter how often you've been stripped at checkpoints.

Bartee used to work as an accountant. 'Oh,' he says, when I start my minidisc, 'there's a lot of technology in today's world, isn't there?' before confusing me thoroughly with a long explanation about the intricacies of Excel spreadsheets. Moses worked for the Ministry of Agriculture in Grand Gedeh county. Now they're both perched on the entrance board to an empty booth. Behind them, someone is listening to a radio; somewhere, all over the camp, someone is listening to a radio. No self-respecting refugee can be without one. I can't hear exactly what's going on, just snippets of news, like 'sporadic shooting', and 'latest fighting'. Nothing unusual.

In 1990 Moses ran away from the NPFL. But they arrested him and his eighteen-year-old brother, and took them to a military base. 'They slaughtered my brother with a knife. Right in front of me. I know who did it – it was General Brooks from Nimba county.' Moses survived because the rebels brought in a haul of captured Krahn men – 'Look!' they said. 'Look at all these monkeys!' – and one of the NPFL men turned out to be an old school friend, and released him.

I've heard a lot of bad stories by now, and I've believed them all. But the UNHCR woman's warning bothered me. 'They'll tell you what you want to hear,' the official had said. Who wants to hear this? Not Moses; his hands are shaking and he's uncomfortable. Even so, there's a relatively happy ending. He found his family when he registered as a refugee in another Ivorian town, and he managed to pick himself up. 'I built one house, then another house, then a third house. I did plantation work and swamp rice farming. It was a UNHCR farming project; they gave me land and seeds and tools. Then the Ivorian crisis stopped me. The Ivorians just took my land and gave it to Ivorians. After that, I came here.'

Now it's Bartee's turn. When he first became a refugee, he worked for Caritas up in the Taï region. Then the LPC crossed over and started killing Ivorians. Ivorians retaliated by killing Liberians. Lists were drawn up. 'They wanted me because I was a prominent person, because I was head of Caritas there. But what saved me was that my house didn't look like a refugee house. They were looking for shacks made of bush materials. I lived in a nice house, which I shared with the deputy mayor of Taï.' For four hours he hid in the kitchen, away from the windows. Four hours were enough to give him a heart complaint from which he still hasn't recovered.

Bartee wants to tell a joke. 'It was so funny; after we got in the bush we got on the main road, and I was carrying my baby on my shoulders because my wife couldn't carry him any more. There was a group who wanted to search us. There was this thought that if you have a baby on your back they will not shoot you, so my wife said, "Give me my son!" I said, "No! He's been with me, I been carrying him!" She said, "I want to put him on my back." I said, "But he's not falling off!" Afterwards we confess to each other, and I said it was better for me to keep the child because she was a woman, and they rarely kill women. If I had the child, they would not kill me.' Moses and he are laughing at this. I am laughing. He says, 'So. They were terrible times.'

Bartee got safely to Tabou, but a young Ivorian man recognized him in the street. By this time the Ivorian head of the armed forces, General Robert Guei, was saying publicly that he didn't want to see any more Liberians. He meant he didn't want to see any alive, and Ivorians were following his orders. The young Ivorian man told Bartee he would kill him, sooner or later. Suddenly, Liberia seemed safer, even though this was 2000 and there was fighting there too.

'I started working on an oil-palm project that was managed by some Belgian firm. By the end of the year Charles Taylor took the company away from the legal owners and gave it to his Lebanese friends, because they were the ones importing his things. Especially his war tools. They would ship them in. They were doing logging as well, so the ship comes in with things and goes back with logs.' Then the logs were sold for more 'things'. In 2002 a Global Witness report called 'Logging Off' said timber had replaced conflict diamonds (diamonds sold by combatants to raise money for weaponry) as the main funding for Liberia's wars. They called it conflict timber, because it was as blood-soaked and dirty as diamonds ever were.

Bartee was in charge of statistics and analysis. So he knew about shipments. And he knew that the Lebanese owners of the company, in return for Taylor's favours, had to pay 'pocket money' to the country's institutions. Police, government employees, soldiers: none of them were getting salaries by now, so they needed to be kept happy. 'They wanted me to do gymnastics with the tax returns. They were looking for a way not to pay taxes, because they thought they were providing enough services to the government already. They didn't think taxes mattered to the big man.'

But then in 2003 MODEL started attacking. The company's military adviser – all the big plantations had nasty militias – advised Bartee to leave, quickly, because he knew too much. 'But I couldn't come to Ivory Coast then because there were rumours going round that these guys who were here were threatened. There was a rumour that men were not being allowed into Ivory Coast. It came to the point where staying in Liberia was a devil; coming to Ivory Coast was a devil, but coming to Ivory Coast was the better of two devils.'

He paid $10,000 Liberian (about £100) to get his family out of the house and to the border. At the waterfront they were stuck. 'There were a lot of government soldiers still there. I was listening to my radio and I said, "Oh, Monrovia has fallen!" and everybody paid so much attention to that, they decided to go back to Harper to find out if it was true. I didn't pull it out of the blue sky; there had been some skirmishes. Anyway, that gave me [the idea] to come across.' His wife went ahead to rent a house in Tabou. 'I had learned my lesson, about not being close to the border. We paid 52,500 CFA to get a place on a truck, but when we got to the junction at Tabou, the locals were enraged. The military detained us and said we should go back to Liberia. But they talked and talked and compromised and we came to the camp. So we never made it to our house in Tabou.'

Tabou is one kilometre away. But it may as well be a hundred. 'I can't move there. The hostility has become a scar. Lately, the scar has been partly removed, but it can still open up again.'

Ahmadou Koné picks me up one Monday morning and he's fuming. 'They killed a young boy! They beat him to death!' It happened the day before, and it wasn't pleasant. The story, according to several rumours, goes like this: a boy had given his sister's mobile phone to his friend. The sister went to her friend, a captain in the military, to rectify the situation. The captain sent some of his 'elements', who beat the boy to death, in broad daylight. The case has upset the town – the IRC workshop staff, on the way to Nero Village, spend most of the trip having a deafeningly animated discussion about it. Koné and Simon-Pierre want a judicial enquiry; the women want to organize a sit-in protest. There is more political awareness and passion than I've ever heard in a carload of my peers.

The case has also unnerved Liberians. Every refugee knows about the story, because they are attuned to anything that ripples their calm, and this incident qualifies. They are jumpy, because another incident three weeks before my visit had prodded and poked the scar. 'All the Liberians were an inch away from getting thrown out,' an aid worker tells me. It was a dangerous moment, and it arose from an incident that exposed all Tabou's fault-lines. A Liberian boy had beaten up his Liberian girlfriend. Instead of seeking redress through the UN system or refugee committee, as she could have done, she went to the Ivorian military and complained to them. Tabou's refugees still shake their heads at this. What was she thinking? (Maybe, reasonably, that the Ivorian judicial system pays little heed to refugee complaints.) The Ivorian military called in the local Guéré fighters, the not-very-former vigilantes who a year earlier had pushed out the rebels and attacked Liberians. The vigilantes punished the boy, and he went to the Ivorian police. 'This opened up old wounds between the Guéré and the police, which dated from the war.' The refugee who is telling the tale won't go on the record. He can't afford to. 'In Liberian custom you say when you pull the rope, the rope will pull the bush and under the bush you will find snakes. The girl pulled the rope. The police and the Guéré went into a clash. Confidentially I can tell you . . . is that [my minidisc] recording?'

I switch it off. 'The police haven't fought any war so for them the whole thing was a nightmare. The Guéré still think they control the area, but the police decided to take a stand against jungle justice. The case went to court. The boy was in prison for three months and had to pay 100,000 CFA. Since then the local population has said officially that no Liberian is allowed in the bushes to take wood.'

Things weren't always this bad. After the really bad times, in May, relations had improved. There was intermarriage, dating, things that soothe. But when the Guéré confronted the police, Tabou blamed the Liberians for causing trouble.

'They are angry with us,' says Bartee, 'because war took place in Grebo and Liberians were involved in it. But let me tell you a story: when you train a dog to hunt, you take some pepper and put it in his mouth and make him eat rice crust. Then you go into the bush. When you fail to take him hunting, he will eat your chickens. Today Ivorians are blaming us, but who trained Taylor's forces? They used to pass through here. Doe had murdered [Côte d'Ivoire's president] Boigny's son-in-law.

So you train him to fight, he fights and he comes back and eats the chickens.'

But Bartee isn't going back anytime soon. 'There is light in the tunnel, but I'm not sure how big the beam is. If there is to be settling of scores back there, then I prefer to die in this fence. I'd rather be killed by an Ivorian.'

Later, when I'm visiting the booth called New Jersey City, I find Bartee sitting on a bench. He shares New Jersey City with the Wilson family, but there's no name painted on his side of the booth. 'I don't have impossible dreams,' he says, as his family swirl around his feet. A trained agriculturist, living in zinc.

I'd met Comfort Wilson at the Magic System circus. She was wearing a GBV workshop T-shirt, and she insisted on talking to me. She had a story. There are twenty people in her family, and all of them live in the 15 square-metre confines of New Jersey City. There are three generations of family here, from Comfort's mother down to someone's son Blessing. They've partitioned the space into four rooms, all scrupulously neat, with shoes hanging on the walls and even a clothes rack. They've managed to get mattresses – UNHCR only provides mats – and Comfort sleeps on hers with four children. Her niece Rose sleeps with seven, on two mattresses pushed together. She shows me how: sideways, so the children fit on, but her feet hang off.

UNHCR didn't provide partitions, either, but many refugees have got them from somewhere. They are made out of tarpaulin and sticks, and they have padlocks and signs saying 'Please knock when you enter.' (How to knock on a piece of tarpaulin: splay your fingers and pat the plastic.)

Comfort has written her story down. She's going to send it to UNHCR, and she's taken time over it, which is something she has in abundance. Four pages long, double-sided, with headings. It reads like a dress rehearsal of an immigration interview.

> *Why you left Liberia?*
> I narrowly escaped because I was tortured and almost killed because of my position held in Liberia as a senior adviser in Maryland County Concerned Women's Committee. I was accused of being a saboteur of the plan for Taylor's security men [to attack Tabou].
> *Why you cannot return home?*
> Because the very Taylors men who did tortured me and are still hunting for me are all mixed with the new interim government and will still wish to accomplish their mission to eliminate me.
> *Why you cannot stay here in Côte d'Ivoire?*
> Because of the in and out of Taylor's men. They threatened me once in Maneke village on 21st October 2003. So if I open my mouth to anything they would do anything to me.

Comfort has scars to prove her story: she was taken to a barracks, she says, and beaten with a cartridge belt. 'They said they were waiting for their commander, William Toe.' But MODEL soldiers arrived before Toe did, and she escaped. She tells me she can't leave the camp to go to Tabou, because she's too scared, but when I come to find her the next day, she's gone shopping to Tabou. I feel bad for disbelieving her, but I get a little cynical. And I think of an immigration officer, hearing such tales all day every day, and can understand why such details can influence a decision. I don't like it, but I can understand it.

Tabou has a beautiful beach. It's pleasant in the evening, with a Flag beer and peanuts and the lighthouse flashing: I see why

Côte d'Ivoire had a good tourism industry, until it was wrecked. Still, the hotels here are doing good business. Probably better than before, as foreign humanitarians have more disposable income than foreign hippies.

I stay for a while in the pink hotel – I never grasp its name – run by Madame Rosalie. She is large, warm-natured and omnipotent. Her son says, one evening. 'There is no food and no drink,' but I was asking the wrong person: Madame Rosalie produces fried chicken and potatoes, and there's always a Flag.

But even Madame Rosalie is powerless in the face of Tabou's shortcomings. When I had just arrived, I marched in outrage out of my room and said, 'But there's no running water!' She had merely smiled. There's no running water in Tabou, Madame. Hasn't been for a while. Don't you have two buckets-full in the bathroom? I do, and the next morning I see where it comes from; two young women at the hotel spend an hour walking to and fro to the well to fill the hotel's tank. This is the equivalent moral prod to those hotel cards pleading you reuse your towels. Except there are no towels in Tabou either. 'I asked someone to go and buy some,' says Jennifer, 'and they came back with used ones. Used towels! That's all they sell.' But Tabou is not a poor town. There is a bustling market, and there are plantations. It should have better facilities by now.

'It's been a problem since the refugees came,' says Madame Rosalie, though with no bitterness. It's just what happened. A small seaside town became a mass refuge. Tabou's population quadrupled in a couple of months, and the water system couldn't cope. Now, there's running water for fifteen minutes a day, on a good day. The usual things happened, when a refugee influx takes place: prices soared. There was some resentment. The French bakery – Ivorians like their baguettes – broke down more often than usual. The UNHCR campaign is wishful, not realistic. Refugees indeed have problems, but they cause problems too. But at the same time, and this also usually happens, refugees were good for business. 'People had closed businesses,' says Simon-Pierre. 'They'd shut up their houses and bars and gone to Abidjan. Now they've opened the bars again and it's very hard to find housing.' The monthly rent for a room used to be 5,000 CFA a month. Now it's 15,000 CFA. Even local NGO workers – on better salaries than most, though a fraction of an expat pay packet – are having trouble finding accommodation.

Some of them stay at le Campement, down the track from the pink hotel. Everybody wants to stay here, because it looks onto the beach. Once the Prestige bar next door is done playing very loud music, you can sleep to the sound of the waves. No running water, a fuzzy-screened television in the bar, but still the best hotel for miles. But the rooms are impossible to get because aid workers snatch them up, and the aid workers are increasing in number, now that Tabou has finally been designated a priority refugee zone. Before, the priority zone was Guiglo, where Peace town is, but they only ever had four thousand refugees up there. That was nothing, compared to Tabou.

Save the Children is increasing its staff. IRC opened its Tabou field office in late 2003, and already needs to expand. The only organization left understaffed and underbudgeted is UNHCR, with only nine staff to deal with 40,000 people. The organization that is supposed to benefit from the generosity of nations is the worst-off. At every village I go to near the border, refugees say they haven't seen UNHCR for months. It's physically and financially impossible to do everything that should be done. In 2002 UNHCR asked for US$163 million from donor nations for the Côte d'Ivoire programme, and they were given a third of it.

★

These are unusual times for UNHCR. Their attention is focused on the US resettlement programme, which is a very big deal. The US government has asked for 6,000 refugees, though the indications are that they might take 9,000. They want the most vulnerable, the most needy. The tired, the poor, the wretched refuse of the teeming shore. So it is written on the Statue of Liberty, and so the US government has decreed. It is an odd, last-minute decision. In 2001 and 2002 the Bush administration let in only 30,000 refugees. It was 'a very low point in the history of the US Refugee Program', according to the US Committee for Refugees, and closely linked to the September 11 attacks. This Liberian programme is the first big undertaking since September 11. Every Liberian in Côte d'Ivoire is talking about it, even though no one is allowed to talk about it. 'It's top secret,' a senior UNHCR official says. 'You can write about it for a book, but there's to be no immediate media coverage. The first newspaper article, and we'll get Liberians moving from all over West Africa to get on it.'

She's right, of course. In Monrovia a foreign businessman told me some of his staff had moved back from Ghana, because they'd given up hope of getting on the UK resettlement programme. People uproot themselves and run after rumour and possibility, all over the sub-region. The British honorary consul in Monrovia gets dozens of begging letters a day. 'Can I go to England?' 'No.' 'Can I go to England?' '*No!*'

UNHCR is responsible for gathering the refugees and doing initial screenings. I go to the last screening day in San Pedro. The location for the interviews – the Rotary Centre – is a giveaway, because there's a massive crowd of hopefuls outside. I expect it to be the same inside, but the large hall is virtually empty. A dozen or so people – mostly women with children, but some nuclear families – sit on wooden chairs, waiting to present their refugee ID card to the first desk. Their identity is confirmed, and they go to the family desk, which has the job of deciding whether their children are who they say are. I'm not allowed to know more about the family desk than that, puzzlingly, because 'that information is confidential'. Whereas whether they've got measles or malaria is not: there's no problem with my sitting at the medical screening desk, along with two charming and bored Ivorians.

The expansion and contraction of extended families according to who wants to know is what bothers critics of resettlement. 'There are lots of separated families,' says an aid worker. 'You have families that have taken in neighbours' children or separated families, and when they get the chance for resettlement, they dump them. I don't like resettlement.'

Other people don't like it for other reasons. It's a cop-out, a young aid worker says. 'They shouldn't be offering resettlement; they should be trying to sort out the problems in the countries that make resettlement necessary.' There are disagreements about the 'cherry-picking' nature of it. 'They want nice nuclear families, so the applicants make their families fit.' Shave off a niece here, a stray there. There are even rumours of compulsory HIV tests.

I see none of that in the big room in San Pedro. There is certainly selection going on: refugees on this resettlement programme have to have been on a census carried out in 2002, then two follow-up registrations. They have to have an ID card, or convince the UNHCR staff that something unavoidable happened to it. 'They tore it up at the checkpoint,' is as common as 'the dog ate my homework,' but it's undoubtedly true.

There is rejection; many women have set up or had children with Ivorian or Ghanaian men. Even with non-formal marriages, the woman takes the man's nationality. A Ghanaian man comes with his wife and children, and the UNHCR desk officer knows they won't get through, as she sends them to the family desk. 'But that's good. That means the family will stay together.'

There are medical tests performed by the two charming Ivorians at the screening desk, but not for HIV. They test for infectious diseases and temperature. The test they do for malaria seems pretty pointless, when everybody has it. It is the hidden casualty rate of civil war: refugees usually avoid roads, which are likely to be used by the military, so they have to walk through unfamiliar bush and landscapes. Their built-up immunity to malaria doesn't work any more, so they bring malaria with them into the host country. A recent World Bank study reported that, for every 1,000 refugees, the host country sees 1,406 additional cases of malaria. It concluded that malaria has increased in the world, because the number of war refugees has increased.

But there aren't enough people to keep the Ivorians occupied with malaria, so we share grilled bananas and peanuts to pass the time. 'You should have seen this place last week,' says Stéphane, looking at the vast empty space of the hall. 'It was packed!' Even the Ivorian soldier on the door is bored enough to ask me a question. He looks at the final table, where refugees accepted on the convoy to Abidjan are given a plastic bracelet. This is like a golden ticket, but the soldier is oblivious. 'Doesn't it wear off when you wash it?' Maybe all he cares about is that some refugees are leaving. Less hassle, but also less income.

UNHCR were expecting 400 applicants today. By 2 p.m. not even a quarter has turned up, and the trickle of arrivals is slowing. We pack up and go home. 'It's bizarre,' says the UNHCR officer. 'It's the chance of a lifetime and they didn't turn up! We sent the notice out in November. That should be enough time.' Earlier, when she told me not to mention resettlement, she said news of it spread like wildfire. Just not to the villages where the missing 300 refugees are.

★

I phone the UNHCR deputy representative in Abidjan to ask permission to visit one of the resettlement transit centres. He's cheery and helpful. 'We'll have to be careful which one we choose,' he says, down a crackly mobile phone line. 'We don't want you getting beaten up.'

The day I return to Abidjan from Tabou, the refugees had revolted. They gathered outside the UNHCR compound, just off Rue des Jardins, and demonstrated. I found this understandable: they had been accepted onto the resettlement programme by UNHCR, and now American immigration officials had rejected them. 'It wasn't just a few, you know,' says someone at the IRC office. 'There were dozens.' It seems like cruelty to me, to let them get that far and then no further. 'It's hard,' said the UNHCR person in Tabou. 'But we can either choose to do it for 6,000 people or for none. We chose the 6,000, but it's hard.'

In my hotel one morning, I eavesdrop. There's a Norwegian at breakfast who had been at the screening in San Pedro. The rumour is that Norway is planning another resettlement programme of 1,000 people, and they've come to see what's going on with the American one. Not much, this Saturday morning. A man with a ponytail and a UNHCR cap fills them in. 'Our convoy has gone missing. It should be here by now.' That's not the only problem. San Pedro's empty Rotary centre had obviously never filled up again. 'We're supposed to have 500 per convoy. We had 440 on the last one, but we've only got 150 on this one.' The Americans are insisting on a five-week schedule, and he doesn't think they can gather enough people. This is an incredible concept, as almost every Liberian I ever met – except for Cerue at WIPNET in Monrovia, who says scornfully, 'I'm not an America-freak – they don't know how to live' – would willingly move to the US, if it was on offer. But the criteria are strict, and the villages with the people who match the criteria are far and difficult to reach. There are 10,000 refugees who are judged to be vulnerable. There aren't enough places on the programme for the refugees, yet there don't seem to be enough refugees for the places on the programme. 'We've got a tight schedule,' the man says. 'Time is money. They want to do it American-style – fast and mean. Invade Iraq and don't let the UN in until it's too difficult. Then, suddenly, it's a UN problem! Oh, am I betraying my politics?'

There are other problems. Some applicants had gone through their three days of interviews – with the Bureau of Population and Migration, and with IOM (International Organization for Migration) – and been sent to America. By late last year 880 had been flown out, and others were set to follow, when it stopped. 'There was a measles outbreak,' says Julien at IRC. He heard about it from Centers for Disease Control in Atlanta, though one of the transit centres is five minutes from the IRC office.

That's not the one that has been decreed safe to visit. UNHCR's information officer, a relaxed Ivorian called Simplice, has been instructed to take me to the other side of town. Abidjan is a sprawling city, so this takes a while. The journey takes us past the stunningly concrete cathedral, built mostly underground, with stained glass windows of jungle animals. Past the bridges where bodies were piled up, the hotel where Charles Taylor and other assorted crooks stayed.

Eventually, the office blocks turn to less exalted buildings, which turn to markets, which turn to shacks and garbage, and a cement mixer churning out something unpleasant-looking into the river nearby. This is the *quartier sensible* of Marcory Sans-Fil. This translates as Marcory Unplugged, because it didn't have electricity for years. Now it has electricity, and two transit centres filled with hopeful Liberians, who have probably never had electricity before, or hope.

I'm selfishly looking forward to this – happy refugees; satisfied customers. But the transit centre is packed and unpleasant. There is a fog of flies, not enough food, and the same gripes: the roof leaks. There's not enough space. They don't like bulgur wheat. When are they going to leave?

This is a mystery. UNHCR is one of the official implementing partners for the US's Bureau of Population and Migration, but sometimes the information only goes one way. One refugee shows me a 'hold notice'. It says he's being checked out for security reasons, but nothing further. Lots of people have been given these hold notices, he says, but no more information. One step closer to the gate, but the carpet can still be pulled. Simplice doesn't know what the hold notice means, and I never find out.

The majority of the residents have been accepted on the programme. Twelve had been refused, a week earlier. I ask someone to tell about it, but he can't help. 'At the time they were feeling very bad and you cannot even ask them to show you the letter they received. They just kept themselves to themselves, and then they left.'

Everyone else has passed their interviews and done the cultural orientation course, and they're waiting for the measles quarantine to finish. The Waylee family fit all the proper vulnerable criteria. Peter saw his wife's father's head lying on a path, after NPFL had taken over their village. They wrote, 'Knight Killer, we will be back,' on the wall, and that was as good as an arrow pointing Anywhere But Here. ('All Liberians are well trained,' a refugee in Tabou said. 'You see something and you hide.') The Waylees ran to the Cavally river, two days' walk away. There they took some light wood, lashed it together, and floated across. They were lucky: sometimes, refugees tried to cross rivers on foam mattresses. Unsuccessfully, mostly. Susanna was carrying Peter Junior, who was a year old.

They ended up in the town of Taï. A nice name, and an ugly situation. At first things were fine; Susanna is from the Krahn tribe, and the chief of Taï spoke the same language. 'He accepted us,' says Peter senior. 'But certain behaviour we couldn't understand. You buy the land, you pay 20,000 CFA. Then they say you come and brush an acre for them, brush it and then you can brush your own, while you have paid money for it already.' He still sounds puzzled at the unfairness of this. But what can be done? 'After some time, war came down. Liberian rebels came and attacked Taï, and the people in the town started killing Liberians.' They started at two o'clock precisely, after a meeting of the local youth. After four years the Waylees' neighbours picked up their machetes and cut the Liberians. 'They started killing us in the bush, but we managed to get to the next town. They had cutlasses-o.' Liberians call these 'silent weapons'. The next family who come for interview – a troop of Collinses – tell the same story, but more gruesomely. 'They came across for a cross-border raid. The same family we ran away from! So the local population started killing us. They grabbed young men and beat them to death. They used machetes, the local hunting guns. Sometimes, they just tied their hands together and threw them in the river. We saw it happening. My wife's nephew was killed: they saw him on the road, they started cutting him and they left his body there.'

Both the Collinses and the Waylees got to Guiglo around the same time, and, because about four thousand Liberians arrived with them, Peace town camp was set up in the small town of Nicla. Peace town is what the refugees named it, aspirationally. Both families built their own houses by selling the tarpaulin distributed by UNHCR. Jimmy Collins explains how to build a three-bedroom residence: 'You just go into the bush and get more sticks, and it'll take about a month. You have to find food, too, so you can't work on it all the time.'

There was peace in Peace town until 2002, when the war turned up again, Ivorian rebels came to Guiglo on 6 December, and Ivorians started running. So did the internationals, the security, every sense of safety. By 7 December, Peace town was undefended and wide open. All the NGOs had been evacuated. It was probably terrifying. 'Of course it was. The local people wouldn't let us leave. It wasn't safe to go back to Liberia. So we had no other place to go. We just stayed there and waited for a possible massacre.'

I calculate the number of refugee camp massacres I've heard of: Tanzania, Burundi, Congo, Uganda, Shatila. Etc. Did they feel safe? Jimmy Collins raises his hands, makes a gesture. 'Safe, not safe. We had no option. I prayed to God. I said, . . . "If you think I deserve to be slaughtered like an animal, fine. But I don't think I deserve it."' They were lucky. The UN came back after a month and started the resettlement process. Liberians call it 'evacuation'. Some of them think it's salvation.

The Waylees have five people in their family; the Collinses are ten. They fill the small office where I've been housed. So when Barnett K. Barford comes through the door, I hold it open for the rest of his family. There isn't any.

Like everyone so far, he comes prepared with a document folder. ID card, letter of acceptance, maybe a birth certificate. Refugees understand the importance of documentation, because it determines their life or death, sometimes. Another interviewee, Napoleon Toe, was arrested for belonging to a political party and forced to do hard labour on Charles Taylor's family farm for two years. Afterwards, when he decided to escape to Côte d'Ivoire, he carried his university degree and his political party membership card. 'I carried the degree in my hand, because that wasn't dangerous. But the ID card could have got me killed, if any Taylorforces had seen it.' He slit the sole of his shoe and carried it in there, then scuffed and ruined

the shoes so they weren't desirable. There were two vital reasons
for the shoe ruse. 'I knew that if I came to Ivory Coast, I would
have no identity. People could take me for anyone.' And he
understands the documentation needs of the internationals.
'They like to have proof and documentation. So I made sure
to bring it.'

Barnett seems most proud of his certificate confirming that
he's passed the cultural orientation class. He's even brought
his accompanying workbook. It says, 'Describe in your own
words what it means to be self-sufficient.' Barnett says, in his
own words, 'It means that you don't have to rely on someone
while you are capable of doing something for yourself. E.g.,
they told us that there are some agencies that help disabled and
old people and some people rely on them while they are not
disabled. That does not serve self-sufficiency and that wastes
your time because their subsidies do not meet your ambition.
That's it.'

I can see that Barnett will go far. He's already gone a long
way, and he's only twenty-four. 'It's miserable to tell you my
story,' he says, 'but I will tell you.' In September 1990 the war
came to Zwedru, in the sound of *pah-pah-pah* and the *boom-boom*
of mortars. Barnett's father decided to run, and told his two
sons to get ready. Barnett went inside, and was bending down
to tie his laces when the shells fell on the porch where his father
and brother were waiting. He was ten years old. 'The wall
broke and I dropped down because I was badly frightened and
I was badly wounded. My side was cut, and if you wish I can
show you . . .'

No, that's all right.

'No problem. So that's how they died. When I awoke I saw
them lying there in blood. I took a back road and I left.' He
didn't know he was wounded till a gentleman pointed out he
was bleeding. His aunt lived nearby, so he went there. She fixed

the wound with herbs, because there was no medicine, and they crossed into Côte d'Ivoire. When the Taï killings began, they ran again, and his aunt died in the bush. 'I woke up and she didn't move. I had to leave her there.'

He talks calmly now, confidently. His self-possession is almost cocky. But he holds himself like a person who's been alone for a long time. 'I built a two-room house in Peace town, I did my own cooking, my own schooling. I did everything myself.' Not just the basics. You need to do more than that to fill up this much loneliness. On top of finishing secondary school – no mean feat, for an English-speaker in Côte d'Ivoire – he did correspondence courses with the International Bible School in South Africa, with a school in Canada, World English Bible School, World Radio Bible School. Since 1999 he has been studying preaching with the Church of Christ.

Good God, I say. If ever there was someone who should be atheist, it's you. But Barnett can't be caught out. 'It's not God who has forsaken us, it is our own attitude that has justified this – do you understand? Are you getting me? The rocket that killed my family was fired by someone who was misguided: he thought he was just killing Krahn people, but he was offending every Liberian citizen. Because if my father was alive, he would have given certain benefits to me and my country would have enjoyed that. Every citizen has a potential, OK?'

OK.

'Look, I feel lonely all the time. Even at my age, I need a comforter. Someone will come and say, . . . "Oh don't worry about that," but there's no one to help you forget what happened. You need someone to tell something to at a constant time. I won't go back to Liberia because there are still rebels there. If I go back, and there is an outbreak of fighting, and I die, there will be no one alive to tell the story.'

I put the incredible concept to him that someone – say, any

immigration officer, anywhere – might disbelieve his story. That there is such a thing as a fraudulent refugee. That some people believe that almost every refugee is fraudulent. He smiles, because things look very simple from where he's sitting. 'Some people will disbelieve. But any American can believe me, because the fact that I stayed thirteen years in exile – something must be the cause of that, right?'

Even so, he was nervous before his American interviews, like all the families. Rumours had gone round the centre that a huge black American man sat behind a desk and frightened everybody. 'Of course I was anxious,' says Barnett. 'I'd never met a person with the title of US Immigration Officer, and this was a title larger than I could bear. But it was fine! Just like me and you, here, talking.' Mitchell Flomo, another successful applicant, says the same thing. 'I knew there was a chance for me because I told them the real story. They asked me if I would like to learn and I said yes, and that I would like to work for money, and they asked me whether I was a rogue, and I said no. I never had arms. I never. I didn't want to die for nothing. I told the truth and I was successful.' If only things were always that simple.

If the differences between America and Liberia had to be summed up simply, the refugees on the resettlement programme would know what to say: time and utility bills.

'Oh yes,' says Susanna Waylee, who did the cultural orientation programme along with her husband. 'It's very important to be on time in America. There they have buses that have a set schedule. In Africa buses come when they feel like, or they don't come at all. So we have to learn punctuality.'

Other things that they must learn about their prospective country: self-sufficiency at all times (that's where the utility bills come in). Call 911 if there's an emergency (911 is the emergency

number in Liberia, too, but there have been no working ambu-
lances for years, and no working phone exchanges either).
Education is free after the age of five, but you have to pay for
daycare. You have to pay for healthcare too, but that doesn't
seem to have been emphasized much. Everyone will start with
an entry-level job, and they will work hard. Peter Waylee is
expecting to do two jobs; so is Mitchell Flomo. Their wives
will work too, and they will take turns in looking after the small
children. Everybody – father, mother, babies, teenagers – wants
to go back to school.

Susanna is looking forward to something else. 'Also they talk
about the wife and the husband, they have equal rights. In our
society they mistreat the wife because they think she's inferior.
Even if the woman is tired, she's forced to work, fetch things,
do everything.'

After a while I get tired of this. I see a made-up America,
where everyone works, and 32.9 million people don't live on
the poverty line. I get annoyed enough to say to Barnett, 'But
didn't they tell you they have guns in America?' and I feel guilty
when he looks slightly alarmed. 'No, do they?' Private guns, I
say, backtracking. Not everybody. No rebels. 'Oh, yes, they
told us that in the areas where we're going to live, we might
hear gunshots,' says Mitchell Flomo. 'We just have to call 911
and we'll be fine.'

Didn't they mention that there might be racism? That people
might not be welcoming? 'No. They only tell us that when we
get to America, we are all the same. They said, "when you are
there, you are not refugees. You are all one."' They believe it,
and I don't disabuse them. It might turn out to be true. And I
feel ashamed of my cynicism, because the truth is irrelevant.
They don't want the trappings of western life, the luxuries, the
pleasures. They want the basics that we take for granted, like
the right to go to sleep without having a bag packed, or the

concept that they are safe. 'All I want,' says one man, 'is security and school.' They're not expecting to go to heaven. They just want to go somewhere that's better than hell.

# 8. Odyssey

'It is some time since so few have been asked to do so much
for so many on so little.'

(Dr Elfan B. Rees, writing about the UN budget for
Second World War refugees, in 1953)

It is hard to believe that Liberia could ever seem a safe place, but
everything is relative. In November 2002 rebel forces attacked
Danané, at the beginning of Côte d'Ivoire's war. Among the
20,800 Ivorians who crossed into Liberia for refuge was Francis
Fladé Nemlin. He is head of logistics for the IRC's field office
in Tabou. We had said hello, here and there, but nothing more.
I was busy talking to refugees living in the transit centre, to
Liberians living in the Tabou region. I hadn't even noticed
there was an ex-refugee in the office, until Jennifer said I should
talk to him. She said he'd been a refugee in Liberia, and I
thought I hadn't heard her right. But one evening Francis asked
me quietly if I had time for his story. We talked on the porch
under a thunderstorm. It was 7 p.m. and I was tired. It took
him three hours to tell it, because he is methodical, and not a
logistician for nothing. But the three hours passed quickly. And
I hadn't heard wrong.

### Francis Fladé Nemlin's story
### *(see map on pages vi–vii)*

My story is a bit long. I was a logistician for [German aid organiz-ation] GTZ in Danané. I decided to come to Tabou to see my family, on 26 November 2002. There was a lot of tension on the way, so every village had two or three checkpoints, so I had to spend the night at Meyagui, 600 kilometres en route. The next day I set off again and I arrived in Tabou Wednesday, around 3 p.m. The next day, Thursday the 28th, I went to visit my relatives. Then a friend called me from Danané to inform me that Danané had been attacked, that the rebels had already taken over the town. So there was total panic. Then a colleague called me, he said he was at my house, that he'd gone there to hide the vehicles. There was my wife and my four children, and two girls who lived with us, my wife's daughter and niece. The oldest was eight. Then six, three and a half, and my daughter was three months.

I spoke to my family and my wife told me that she'd been coming back from somewhere and she heard shots. When she heard them, she fled looking for the children. She got to the main street, and saw the two girls who were coming towards her, crying. She asked, 'What's happened?' And they said they had left their little brother near the school and they didn't know where he was. She sent them home and said she was going to look for the boy. There were shots being fired left and right, but she carried on, she got to the school, they told her the teacher had taken the children away but they didn't know where. People had fled in all directions. She was in a panic. Luckily, she happened to look in a yard and she could see the teacher there with the children. She knocked on the gate and the teacher wouldn't open up. My wife insisted, she said she wanted to come in and the teacher said no. The town was encircled, the rebels were 800 metres away.

My wife told the teacher she had left her baby daughter, three months old, at the house, and she needed to get her son. She took her son home. She was running through the streets with him, she was exhausted, she got home and they shut the door. For forty-five minutes, one hour, they stayed there. I was calling all day from Tabou, I spent 35,000 CFA (£36) on the phone, I was calling all our relatives, all our acquaintances in Abidjan, Danané, to have some idea of what had happened. I didn't have any favourable responses. In the evening we were listening to the radio, and they told us that rebels were fighting in Danané. I looked in my mobile and found a number for a man I'd worked with in Danané, and I asked him to go and look for my wife in the house. He said, 'Most people have left, anyone who knows the countryside has left, it's a bit difficult to get hold of anybody.' I asked him to go and see whether my family had left or if they were still there. He didn't want to go outside, because there was shooting and killing, but he said he would.

The rebels were mostly Liberian. They had come from Liberia to attack Danané. It wasn't the typical Liberian rebels, it was Liberians who had just joined up. But I didn't see them, so I don't know. Those who told me about it said there were child soldiers, too. Anyway, the man went to look, and I kept phoning. He arrived in the yard and luckily there was a young man who had already run away, but who had come back to get something, and the man asked him where the family had gone to. The young man said they'd gone in that direction. The man asked him to ask my wife to do her best to come back into town because her husband had phoned from Tabou. She told me later that when the young man gave her the message, he also told her that there were rebels on the road, and when there is a woman travelling, they will take all your money. She said, OK, but I'm going.

She got to the house and came on the phone and we decided that as she didn't know any of the countryside round there she would follow all the people who were heading for Liberia. We agreed I would call the next day to see if she had any more information. The next day, the phones were dead. The landlines, the cell phones didn't work. [He laughs.] So I was there not knowing where my family was. I had to go and look for them.

I couldn't pass through Guiglo because the rebels had a position and our loyalists had a position, so they didn't even let you pass. And it wasn't a good idea to go to the rebels when no one was sure who they were. Seeing as I'd told my wife to go towards Liberia, I thought maybe I could pass through Harper and then try to ask the NGOs if they could help me. I knew that GTZ were there, and UNHCR had a little office there, which they'd set up to prepare for the crisis.

So I applied for the laissez-passer from the police. I should say that I was really scared about going to Liberia. There was fighting there too. It wasn't LURD, they were in the north, but the government forces in the south had an attitude that was unacceptable. People were constantly being threatened. The day I arrived at the border, at Prollo, the same day, our army had destroyed the barge so that Liberians couldn't cross, because we had information that most of the rebels were Liberians. I crossed, if I remember correctly, a week after the events. It was a Saturday. At the border, people were telling me that there were police on the road, but I decided to cross anyway. I took a pirogue. I paid 1,000 francs [£3]. I showed my laissez-passer.

They said I couldn't pass because it hadn't been signed at the border. I told them there was no one there to sign it. I said I didn't have time to go and look for anybody. I had to negotiate and pay money, and I crossed.

When I got to Harper, I was helped by a local NGO who were at the border to meet Liberians who were crossing back. They gave me a lift. As I'd worked for IRC and we'd set up an office in Harper in 2000, people knew me. Luckily I found a Liberian refugee who I'd known in Côte d'Ivoire and I explained my problem to him. The next day I went to the immigration office so they could call the other border crossing at Lokako. We tried to call, but it was impossible. The next day I went back and we called. I went to the [UN]HCR office as well and found some GTZ people who had come from Monrovia. I went to them and gave them my GTZ ID card. I explained my situation to them, but they didn't really pay me any attention. I asked them to send a message to Monrovia to see if they could help me and they gave me the impression they could do it but then nothing happened. They'd say, 'We can take you to Monrovia and you can look for your family,' and it went on and on. I'd already been in Harper four days. I speak quite good English – I can sound like a Liberian, if I try – so I tried to get information from people. People tried to tell me which roads to take. I said to myself finally that I was already in danger, I was already taking risks, so why not take some more?

On the Friday I set off and spent the night in Plibo, which is 35 kilometres north of Harper. I arrived at the station and I didn't know where I was going to be able to sleep, and a man came towards me and said he had known me in Côte d'Ivoire. I explained that I was looking for my family and didn't know where to spend the night; he said he would send me to someone. He was an Ivorian refugee who was in Liberia. In Liberia, at Harper, I'd worked a bit for UNHCR so a lot of refugees knew me. Where I was staying, two people went out at 9 p.m. and found that a car had arrived from Monrovia. They told him there was a man who wanted to go to Monrovia, but I only wanted to go because I had no idea where my family were. I couldn't go to Lokako because I didn't know the road very well. I'd been to Monrovia in 1998 for some work business, so it's the only place I was more or less familiar with. So I took my bags and came to the station, I asked for different prices, but I didn't have enough to get to Monrovia, I asked at least to go to Ganta, because it's a crossroads town on the roads from Danané, Guinea and Monrovia. They wanted $1,500 Liberian [about £12], but I didn't have enough so I paid $1,100. We set off in a Kia, a car that farmers use. That's what they use for taxis over there. When we left I had my GTZ ID card where my nationality wasn't written down so at every checkpoint I showed that one. I didn't want people to know who I was.

In the vehicle there were Liberians who were talking about the treatment they'd received in Côte d'Ivoire, and they were saying, 'The Ivorians treated us bad, and now the Ivorians will come here and see how they get treated!' I listened but I didn't say anything, even though I had a lot to say. Someone had told the driver who I was so he knew more or less. We'd left at 9 a.m. and we got to Zwedru at 8 p.m. I thought we would spend the night there, but to my great surprise the driver said he wanted to continue. I said, OK. There was a young lady who came up to me saying, 'Why don't you talk, why are you so calm, why don't you eat?' I think she was suspicious. I said, no, it's nothing, it's the first time I've done a trip like this, that's all. I didn't want to speak because I didn't want them to find out who I was.

Of course, there were problems en route. When we got to a frontier point, the soldiers would demand money. They would load drugs onto the vehicle. Big bags full. It was night so I don't know what the drugs were. That was their business. Once we arrived in a village, and someone got on and said, 'Listen, I'm not here, we have to get through the checkpoint.' At checkpoints there were already so many discussions, and we had to beg forgiveness so much to get through them. I had fear in my belly, because I thought, there's a crisis at home and if people discover who I am, anything can happen. So I had to make an even bigger effort to keep quiet.

At 2.30 a.m. we arrived at Ganta. The driver told me I could get down, but I didn't know where to go. I asked if there was a hotel. He said where to go, but it was far away, and he had to continue to Gbarnga. I set off, but I couldn't find it. After two kilometres, I didn't realize I'd already passed it because the driver's description was nothing like the reality. I saw a man approaching and said to myself, What shall I do? It's nearly 3 a.m., if I stop him, he might be a rogue. But I told myself again that I was already taking risks, so I could take one more. He accompanied me to the hotel. I knocked on the door of the hotel and the manager opened and I said I wanted to stay and he said, no, there are no rooms. I said, 'OK, listen, I have no choice, I can stay on your doorstep till morning but I'm not setting foot outside again because it's my first time here and I don't know anybody.' I asked for his forgiveness. He said, 'OK, I can give you my mat but you have to pay $500 [Liberian, about £5]. I said, 'Can I pay $100?' He said, OK.

My body, my nostrils, they were covered in dust. I couldn't sleep because I had the impression that there were people wandering round the hotel, and I didn't know their motive. So I didn't sleep. At 5.30 I got up. In the hope that I might find a transit centre where I might find some people I knew from Danané, I went out and asked the first person I saw if there was a transit centre. He said, 'No, everyone who comes here goes to Monrovia.' I didn't know what to do. But I hadn't eaten the day before and I was very hungry, so I went to get a coffee. While I was having my coffee, two security people came and took away a man who was sitting right next to me. There were discussions, and they told him to follow them or they'd do him harm. I thought this was so weird. There was no reason for it. I said to myself, OK, they took the first person they saw, maybe I'll be the second. So I left.

The town was packed with armed men. So I was forced to be careful so I didn't get discovered to be an Ivorian. But I didn't know where else to go, because I calculated the distance to Monrovia and I knew that if I didn't find the family and had to come back, I didn't have enough money. I had a cousin who worked with an export company in Liberia, in Buchanan. He had his family in Danané too, so I thought he might have an idea what to do. I called him, but he wasn't there. They told me to call back at three, so I went for a walk. At three, my phone battery went dead. So no more phone calls!

I couldn't decide what to do. I could try to get to Lokako or Saniquelle, maybe they'd gone through there. But I decided in the end to go towards Danané, maybe they'd fallen behind. I went to the station, they said it was $500 Liberian to go that way. I begged for forgiveness and asked if I could pay $400. They said no, but I could pay $450. I paid at two o'clock and we waited there until 5 p.m. An old taxi arrived, what we call wora-wora here. We were eight people in the car and eight people on the roof!

The road was really bad. When we arrived at a checkpoint, we had to get down, introduce ourselves. I was still giving them the GTZ ID card. But the checkpoint people would say we still had to satisfy them, so we had to get out some money. Sometimes you pay $50 Liberian, or 1,000 CFA which is $60. Sometimes $100. It depended. So at every checkpoint we got down, apologized, paid and set off. At 7 p.m. we arrived in Kahnple. I didn't have any plan, I'd just left with some idea of finding my family and if not, coming back. But I was going to get stuck because I didn't have enough money. When I left I'd taken 100,000 CFA [£100], but with all the checkpoints and travel, I'd already spent 65,000. Already I didn't have enough to get back. At Kahnple the first thing I asked was where to find a hotel. Someone showed me a hotel. But I asked some other people where they were going and they said the transit centre. I said to myself, Ah! I'll go and have a look, to see if I could meet anyone who had met my family.

The transit centre was made of tents that had been built by UNHCR. When you went into a tent, there were so many people that they were on top of each other, head next to feet, feet next to head. Some people slept outside. They were Ivorians and Liberians who had been in Côte d'Ivoire and who had come back. I wandered around a bit. Seeing as I had some idea about refugee organization, I went up to a woman to ask her what to do. She told me that there were team leaders who had the list of everybody in the camp, and if you're looking for someone they can tell you. At that point someone came up and hit me. I was so tired and nervous and angry and I said in English, 'Why are you touching me?' and I heard, 'Pardon, monsieur.' It was the first time I'd heard French in such a while, so I turned around and somebody just jumped on me. It was my wife's niece. She yelled, 'Uncle is here! Pappy is here!' All my family was in that tent, my cousin's wife, their family. I saw my wife. She said, 'How did you get here?' and I said, 'It's a bit difficult to explain, I did my best to find you and I'm very happy.' At that point I realized what a distance I'd travelled.

So I'd found my family, and now I had a thought in my head that I'd found them, and I was happy, but how would we get back to Tabou? We'd have to do the same itinerary.

The next day my wife told me how she'd got there. She told me that when she'd got into town, she'd gone to the man's house, and he had told her that they were killing people, and that staying in his house wouldn't protect her. The rebels had gone to my house and asked the children where their father was, and they said he was travelling. They said, OK, don't be frightened, we're here to protect you. When my wife went back, she heard this and decided to leave. They spent two days in the man's house, then another man came to discuss with his friend, and said he wasn't confident and was going to Liberia because if not things might get dramatic. My wife heard this and asked the man questions about leaving. The other man came back that evening and said if she could pay him, he would help her. With all the children and my cousin's family, they were sixteen people, including six children under eight years old. The man said he would come back the next day and they would leave at 5.30, because they'd be stopped if they travelled in the daytime. So my wife went to find some couscous to take with them. She had a bit of money. They told her she would have to pay 35,000 CFA [£36] to get to the border. When they left they kept meeting rebels, who were beating up people, telling them that they had stolen stuff.

The man intervened because he and the rebels were the same tribe.

They walked from 6 a.m. to 6 p.m. They decided to spend the night in the village at the border. They had some bags and when they woke up, the bags were gone. Now they wanted to leave urgently, especially as the commander of the rebels was there. He wouldn't let them leave. The man wanted to negotiate to get their possessions back, but my wife said it would make things worse and anyway it was only stuff. She had to pay the rebels and they set off. They walked to the border. It was about 40 kilometres. The children were tired and they had swollen feet, but they had no choice. They crossed at Boutouo, in canoes, which cost 5,000 CFA [about £5]. They spent two nights on the Liberian side of the border sleeping in the open air. She went up to the people who were transporting refugees and showed them my card and said I worked for GTZ and could they help her? They said no. The third day, she went up to a driver who worked for GTZ Liberia and asked if he could help her, the children were sick, their feet were swollen. He said he was sorry, but he really couldn't. She said, 'OK, never mind. I'll leave it up to God.' And when she said this, it really touched him, and he came back and said, 'Why did you say that?' and she said, 'I have to leave it to God, because I can't force you to help us.' He told her to give him the list of the children and he said there were too many. She said, 'Well, that's who I have.' They stayed four or five days there, and the man drove them to Kahnple, where I found them.

But now I had to find a way to get them back. I discussed it with UNHCR who said it was really difficult, that they couldn't take us to Maryland, so we had to stay there until 31 December. By then, I'd been travelling for two weeks. I had no solutions so we said, OK. I asked UNHCR to drop us at Ganta, because I was hoping for some kind of miracle. They said people were going to Monrovia and they could drop us there. But I thought, I have sixteen people with me, where will we stay in Monrovia? So on 1 January we left Kahnple and went to Ganta with HCR.

At the transit centre I'd met an IRC driver who I'd known at Guiglo in 1999. He told me that he had a room we could use in Ganta, that we should talk to his friend who would let us use it. When we arrived, the man told us that someone was using the room already. I said, 'OK. Really, I've got sixteen people, and I don't even have enough money to house them in a hotel for one night. Either we sleep outside or . . . I don't know. I don't have a solution.' I begged forgiveness, and he could put us somewhere. We had been given bulgur wheat in Kahnple and we carried it into the room where we stayed. There were sixteen of us in one room. It was tight!

We started to prepare some food, and I continued to think about how I could get out of the situation. I had taken risks and let HCR take me there but I couldn't count on HCR any more except to get to Monrovia. But I didn't want to go to Monrovia because we'd had information that the first Ivorians to go there had been arrested as suspects. They'd been accused of coming to attack the president of Liberia. So I thought I preferred to take a different route. One day, I went to the IRC office, and I saw a driver of GTZ and showed him my ID card, I explained that I was blocked, I had no more money. He said he couldn't help me. I asked him to call his boss to see if he could help, but he said no. I went back again, and I asked him to forgive me and to call his boss. He called him, and I introduced myself but his boss was annoyed, and wanted to know who I was, where he'd found me, who'd given me his name, all that kind of thing. So the driver was annoyed.

I went home and the driver followed me, and he saw all the children – three months old, two years old, three years old, five years old, eight years old. I said, 'See, I have no choice.' The driver asked me to follow him back to the office. I see a man coming towards me. He lifts me up with a big hug, and I see it's a colleague of mine from GTZ who I knew in Danané. He'd been sent there on a mission. He said, 'You officer, what are you doing here? Are you really a refugee?' I said, 'Why not? It's possible. It happens to everybody, why not me?'

It was him who'd been on the phone. He'd been on the road, that's why he was annoyed. He asked me what I was doing there. I told him I was a refugee, I was fleeing the war, and I was trying to get back to Maryland; then we could get to Tabou. I told him I had sixteen people with me. He said, OK. He phoned the IRC boss, told me I needed a manifest to travel, that he was going to help me because I worked at GTZ. He asked me if I had money, I said no, only a little. He took $1,000 Liberian [£10] and said sorry he didn't have more. It was more than enough. We set off again at 5 p.m. and we got to Zwedru at midnight. We slept there; there was an old military camp which they'd turned into a transit centre.

The next day, they asked for my documents and I said UNHCR hadn't given me any and I hadn't been able to go to Monrovia with UNHCR because I didn't have enough money. They said, OK, and gave us some biscuits for the children. At 9 a.m. we set off for Maryland and at 9 p.m. we got to Plibo where we got off. There were so many checkpoints and so many kinds of people were on the truck; they were armed, but we had to accept them. No one could say anything because you couldn't know what their reaction was. So we had to stay there with them, in fear. It was hard to know who was a soldier, who was a rebel. They were in uniform but it was still hard to tell. Everything was mixed up. There was no difference between them. Even when we were in Kahnple, there were young men coming from Danané, fifteen-year-olds, and they'd tell about how they'd fought in Danané. They'd said, 'Yeah, we went and attacked, and the French army pushed us back but we'll go back and push them back.' At Kahnple I saw my motorbike that I'd used in Danané, that a rebel had brought across. But I didn't say anything. I couldn't.

Anyway, people came and told stories, that some people came

over with TVs, possessions. They were just emptying everything.

In Plibo they told us that rebels had attacked Neka. I was shattered by this because Neka isn't very far from Tabou. The rebels were progressing towards Tabou. So we were stuck in Plibo for two months, waiting. There was too much tension. People crossing over gave us news. Rebels had attacked Neka and there were Liberians there and they were coming over, along with Ivorians. And in Tabou they saw that Liberians were coming down and that caused a lot of tension. They said, 'We let in the refugees and then they join the rebels and attack us!' People said they recognized Liberian refugees amongst the rebels, refugees who had been living in Grebo and Neka, they'd mixed themselves in amongst the camp. Now the local population was totally overwhelmed and they took it out on the refugees. A lot went back to Liberia. They weren't allowed to move around in Côte d'Ivoire. According to the news, refugees who set off along the roads were blocked and attacked. It was really bad.

So we were there, waiting. We were in my friend's house, where I'd stayed on the way north. Sixteen of us. They were very generous. But we went to register at the transit centre. We'd sleep in the house at night and spend the day at the transit centre, so we could qualify for food.

Being a refugee was really, really awful. I'd started thinking like that in the camp in Kahnple. I'd think that only two weeks before, when I lived in Danané, I'd had access to bottled water, a TV, a video. I had a motorbike and a 4WD. And I ended up in a refugee camp without bottled water, without anything. It was depressing. But I forced myself to go on.

In the camp it was so hot I couldn't sleep, there were so many people, and I would think about when I worked with refugees in 1997, and I finally realized then how much refugees suffer. All that time I'd spent working with them, distributing their food, telling them to come back later, now it happened to me. It was hell. All that time, I probably had one hour of sleep and the rest of the time I was thinking. Thinking, thinking, thinking. In Plibo, things were even worse. It took a month to get registered, so it was really awful, having to find food for sixteen people. But we managed, because I'd bought a sack of rice from someone I'd known in Côte d'Ivoire. But that doesn't last long amongst sixteen people. So most of the time we made sure the children ate first. In Danané my baby daughter was used to drinking bottled water, and eating baby food. In Kahnple there was no more food for her. It was a problem. We had to give her CSB [high-energy corn–soy blend] biscuits. So I was really worried about her. She nearly died in Plibo. She was so ill, she was passing water every five minutes. She had diarrhoea for two weeks, and she was malnourished. Someone pointed out to us an old nurse who had worked with Firestone, but he was ill and it was difficult for him to give injections. He told us it was really serious. We wanted to send her to Harper, but it would have been the same thing and in Harper there was already malnutrition. So the nurse really helped us, he gave us the name of the medicine, he said to give it to her for four days and if there was no effect, then there was no hope. The fourth day, she got better. At that point, I had to recognize the power of God: because of everything I'd done and got through, maybe God was looking after me.

All the time I was in Plibo, I had a little radio I listened to. Then we had news that rebels had attacked Neka and that they were in the area. I had no news from my family in Tabou, because everyone was disoriented. Everyone was waiting for the rebels to arrive; there was total panic. Another thing that really bothered me, was that people were passing through with looted materials from Côte d'Ivoire, and I thought of all the things I'd lost and that hurt me. But then I realized there was no point dwelling on it, and that God would help me the next day. So every day at 6 a.m. we got up and prayed. Every day. We asked God to help us, to help Liberia and Côte d'Ivoire. They were both in trouble.

Some Liberians said that there were some Ivorians who had treated them badly, but most had not. Others said that now we would undergo the same suffering they'd had in Ivory Coast. It was a kind of revenge. There were some who were fiercely opposed to the war in Ivory Coast, because they said if there was war there, it would come back to Liberia.

There were French soldiers in Côte d'Ivoire, but they were so few, they didn't exactly inspire confidence. They came and they retreated. Our soldiers couldn't stand up to the rebels. From what I heard, the local people had organized themselves to fight; because they said they weren't in favour of the war, they had to resist the rebels. They managed to hold them off and make them retreat, about 60 km from Tabou. This was in February.

I used to listened to the BBC Afrique at 6 a.m. At 6.30 I listened to RFI. From 9 a.m. I listened to Africa Numéro Un. At 17.30 it was BBC again. So I'd just do a tour of the stations to try and find out what was happening, to find something that was reliable. Then I'd tell my family what was happening. We'd just say that God would help us, because we had nothing else to do.

One day, the HCR protection officer was there, and he said I could be useful to him, because they needed a logistician. I said, OK. That gave me a little bit of hope so I could forget a little bit my troubles. Just for someone to recognize that I could be of use, that might mean that one day I could go back to work.

But now MODEL was pushing from the other side and they were nearing Harper. In March I went over [to Côte d'Ivoire] to see what was happening. I spoke with a few people, wandered around, listened to what people were saying. I'd listen to the people who'd come back from the front. I realized that the rebels weren't yet in a position to counter-attack, so I was reassured. In May I decided to go to Abidjan to see how things were going. It wasn't easy to get there, because you need money. But I saw an ex-colleague. He asked me where I'd been but I said it would take too long to tell him. He lent me 10,000 CFA, because I had nothing left. There was a woman who I gave some money to when I could, and she gave me some clothes. My family had some clothes, but the rebels kept ripping them from them.

Then I saw IRC. In Côte d'Ivoire! I was surprised. In 2000 I'd set up their office. I decided to send applications to various agencies. At that point rebels had arrived in Plibo, and my family had to walk from Plibo to the border. They crossed and arrived in Georgetown, which is 10 kilometres from Nero Village. So I came back from Abidjan and I left again for Georgetown. I'd gone home to Tabou, because we'd kept a house there, and my wife had sent a message to people who were coming to Tabou, so they knew where to find me. So I went to fetch my family again. I had no job, but then IRC called me and said they needed a logistician. That was in June. And that was that.

Now, when I do refugee registration, sometimes the refugees get really stressed and angry, so I say to them, 'Listen, I understand what you're going through. I was a refugee and I know what you're experiencing, so please be a little patient, and don't treat these people [doing the registration] as your enemy. If you tell them they're useless, it won't help, so it's best if you calm down.' One woman came and hit me, saying, 'You're eating, and we've got nothing!' I just tried to remember what I'd gone through and I told her she was right. So when they react like that, I understand. I never get angry. I give them my experience, and I try to give them hope to carry on, that they can live better, as long as they're patient and have faith in God. They shouldn't think that people are looking down on them because they're refugees.

I don't tell people my story unless it's necessary. People don't guess – why should they? But it just proves it can happen to anybody. Why not?

# 9. It Can Happen to Anybody. Why Not?

'In Exile . . . for a while.'

(Title of a Canadian 'refugee-simulation' exercise)

Canada used to be world-famous for its generous refugee policy. But lately its welcome has got colder, mostly due to pressure from the US about security and immigration. In 2002 a group of Canadian NGOs thought the political climate was chilly enough to feel the need for a 'refugee-simulation' exercise. The day-long programme called 'In Exile . . . for a while' is supposed to counter preconceptions of asylum-seekers as economic drains or criminals. The simulation has been done by students and church groups. It's yet to be braved by politicians.

The manual below was produced by Canada's Mennonite Central Committee. On 2 April 2003, when Rosthern College in Saskatchewan organized a voluntary 'In Exile' day, sixty-one students showed up on a Saturday. By the end of the day, nearly all of them had formed a group to make blankets for the MCC. Though they live in a chilly country, they realized – after only a day of being shouted at, abused and frightened – that the experience of a refugee is chillier still.

*The Meeting Site* (6.45 a.m.)  Participants should meet at a designated site away from the camp at 6.45 a.m. Roll-call will occur and at this time, each participant will be given a character ID Profile. The participants should be given a few moments to familiarize themselves with the ID Profiles. This ID Profile will be their personal history for the rest of the event. You could create family units for the youth or leave them to create their own family units. Those participants with special dietary restrictions should be visibly indicated (given special armbands) so that Rebels and Military Personnel know not to confiscate food from these youth.

*Storytelling* (7.00 a.m.) After the youth have been given time to read their ID Profiles, ask them to sit down, to close their eyes and to listen to a story. Have someone read a story about refugee life to the youth to set the context for what they will be experiencing throughout the day.

*Chaos* (7.10 a.m.) Immediately after the story, while the youth are still seated with their eyes closed, attempt to create a sense of confusion and chaos for the youth by having a few volunteers shock the youth out of their peaceful state with whistles, air horns and shouting ('They're coming, we have to go! It isn't safe here! We have to run! We have to leave!') while pushing and jostling the youth – herding them out of this location and towards the path or waiting buses. Effectively done, this surprise can create a sense of insecurity among participants, leaving them to wonder what else is coming for the rest of the day.

*Military Checkpoint* (7.45 a.m.) The refugees will continue on the path, either on foot or by bus until they encounter a Military Checkpoint, guarded by Military Personnel. The participants will be lined up, and two Military Personnel will check ID Profiles, and search through participants' belongings until they find luxury items (watches, radios, extra snack food, etc.). These items are kept by the Military Personnel (leaving food with those youth with special dietary restrictions). Some participants can be detained and interrogated – only allowed to rejoin the group on the Exile Walk.

*Group Divisions* (8.15 a.m.)  While at the Military Checkpoint, Military Personnel will divide participants into groups of no more than 20 people. A Group Facilitator will introduce him/herself to the group by telling them that he is a 'Human Smuggler' and that he helps people get to safety – for a price. He/She points out that the youth have no idea where they are headed, and so they are in need of his/her service. He/She asks for payment in return for this service (watches, earrings, rings, hats, etc.). The Facilitator tells the group that the refugee camp is in another country and that they have to cross the border in order to arrive at the camp. At this point, the refugees will proceed on the Exile Walk in their smaller groups, staggered enough to ensure that they will not see what is happening to the group in front of them. As each group leaves the Military Checkpoint, the remaining youth will continue to be subjected to the harassment, interrogation and searches of the Military Personnel until it is their turn to proceed.

*Exile Walk* (8.45 a.m.)  Each group will go through the same activities and simulations. Some participants can be given extra luggage to carry at this time. Others can be given 'babies' (dolls) and be told that these children are orphans and will die if they do not make it to the refugee camp health and feeding centre.

*Rogue Military Force* (9.00 a.m.)  The youth will encounter a Rogue Military Force along the path, who will ensure that all of the females are veiled. Any of the women who are not veiled will be forced to do so through yelling and intimidation.

*Landmine Simulation* (9.30 a.m.)  Participants will enter a mine-field where dead bodies will be lying and minefield signs will be placed. A simulated explosion will go off (using a noise maker, a tape recording of an explosion or noisy fireworks) and selected participants will be disabled in a variety of symbolic and debilitating forms, from visual and hearing impairment to limb restriction. Visual props such as arm slings, eye patches, ear plugs, crutches and tensor bandages are useful here.

*Rebel Ambush* (10.00 a.m.) After the Landmine Simulation, a group of Rebels will ambush participants, emerging from hidden spots, forcing participants to lie face down. The Rebels will steal from the 'refugees'. The belongings will be returned at the end of the day, but participants should not know this. The Rebels should yell at, intimidate and harass the participants ('You're not welcome here, no one wants you here, go back where you came from!').

*Border Crossing* (10.20 a.m.) When the participants reach the Border Crossing, they will be approached immediately by the Border Crossing Guards who will detain the youth, interrogate them, force them to line up, search their bags and pockets for food or valuables to confiscate, and check their ID Profiles. A number of ID Profiles will be confiscated. The Border Crossing Guards will eventually tell the youth that the Border is closed and that they are not accepting any more refugees. The youth will again have to rely on the 'Human Smuggler' (their Group Facilitator) to guide them to the Refugee Camp.

*Female Abduction* (11.00 a.m.) As participants walk towards the camp, they will encounter a group of several men with weapons who will harass the women and abduct a female (who has been recruited in advance for this role).

*The Camp Gates* (11.10 a.m.) The camp will be guarded by Military. Each group will be forced to wait before they are able to register. The Military will be hostile and intimidating, singling out individuals as 'troublemakers' who will be forced to wait to register until everyone else has been registered.

*Registration* (11.40 a.m.)  Each group will be told that they must fill out the UNHCR forms, and ID Profiles will be checked as forms are distributed. Those youth without ID Profiles will be removed and detained apart from the group. Once the forms are complete, Immigration Officers will conduct interviews with participants, who will have to use their ID Profiles to prove their refugee status. It is very effective if these officials speak to participants only in other languages to simulate arriving in a new country where you do not understand the language. Youth without ID Profiles will be interviewed eventually, before being allowed to join the rest of the group. At this time, men will also be given ration cards for their families.

*The Camp*  Once inside the camp, the men will be told to go to the supply tent to pick up supplies for their families (water, blankets, dishes, tarps or plastic sheets for making shelter, etc.). Lunch will also be provided only to the men, to supply to the rest of their families – rice cakes or something similar, light and easy. You may want to insist that women must be accompanied at all times by a man in the camp, to highlight the danger, inequality and loss of rights that women often face. You can also suggest that this is for their own safety, in order to highlight the dangers specific to women in Refugee Camps.

*Camp Politics/Boredom*  The afternoon can be spent putting up shelters and settling in. Camp Guards and other 'aid' workers could spend this time making 'deals' with refugees, asking for bribes in return for food or medical supplies. Keep in mind that boredom and waiting are a significant part of the Refugee experience, and it is important that the participants experience that as well.

*Rebel Ambush* (4.45 p.m.)  The rebels will ambush the Refugee Camp. They could claim to be seeking to forcibly recruit 'volunteers' to fight in the civil war (this could be used to highlight the plight of child soldiers) or because they are looking for food or other supplies. This ambush is very important to reinforce that even within the Refugee Camp they are not safe.

*Dinner* (5.00 p.m. and 6.00 p.m.) One group will be told that there is not enough food (because it was stolen by the Rebels, or because the supply truck was blown up by an anti-tank mine) and that they will have to wait to eat until there is another shipment. Make the injustice obvious (the other groups are eating while one group is without food). Some time later tell them that the food has now arrived and that they can now eat.

# 10. Phone Home

'If you have not received this letter,
please contact NASS immediately.'

(Extract from a letter sent by the National Asylum
Support Services to asylum applicants)

In a living room in Northampton a woman is looking at me scornfully. 'You want to know about Liberians? People tell so many lies about Africa, why should we talk to you?' And with a *pah!* of contempt, she turns her back.

This is a shock. I've been talking to Liberians for weeks now, but this is only the second time I've been on the receiving end of hostility. It happened first in Tabou transit centre, when a woman walked past me and spat out, at no one in particular, 'We're all refugees, we're all suffering!' She said it with fury, not self-pity.

I explain what I'm writing about, and the woman calms down. She even mutters a 'sorry', and talks about her situation. She laughs about her phone bill, because it's typically refugee in size (large) and content (Monrovia, Accra, Harare). Her manner is conciliatory. But her initial rudeness says more about her life here than her story does.

'The United Kingdom has a proud tradition of providing a safe haven for genuine refugees.' So says the website for the Home Office's Immigration and Nationality Directorate (IND). It goes on: 'The UK Government is determined to ensure that genuine refugees are properly protected and that there is no incentive for people who wish to migrate for other reasons to misuse asylum procedures.'

Ask a Home Office official a slightly controversial question about anything to do with its asylum system – for example, why is it such a chaotic, cruel mess? – and a wounded reply will come back from the press office. This reply will unfailingly mention the precious cultural contribution to the UK made by German refugees fleeing the Nazis, or Ugandan Asians, and by extension, the UK's great generosity in welcoming them. This was true then, and it's still true now, as a historical fact. But times have changed.

Whenever I met a Liberian – in a refugee camp, IDP camp, Northamptonshire living room – they would bid me 'welcome'. But welcome is an unfamiliar concept where I come from. In an ICM opinion poll conducted in 2001, 58 per cent of the British public said they believed that asylum-seekers come to Britain because they want a better life for themselves and their families. This is true, if a better life means not getting shot or shelled. But that's not what the British public meant. A survey a year later by MORI showed what they meant: 64 per cent said the media most commonly used the term 'illegal immigrant' when it talked about asylum-seekers or refugees, while 85 per cent associated negative expressions with refugees or asylum-seekers, such as 'bogus', 'scroungers' and 'foreigners'. Words that weren't associated with them were 'skilled', 'hard-working' and 'welcome'. After 9/11, when suspicion of swarthy foreigners became political currency, and after Special Branch officer Stephen Oake was killed in an anti-terrorist raid on an asylum-seeker's house in Manchester, the newspapers turned asylum-seekers from scroungers into terrorists. The campaign is working: during Refugee Week in June 2003, a MORI poll of 15–24-year-olds found that 58 per cent of them disagreed with the statement 'asylum-seekers and refugees make a positive contribution to this country'.

Such hostility is nurtured, not natural. It is created by the use of clever confusion. Conflate the terms 'economic migrant' and 'asylum-seeker' often enough – in public pronouncements, legislation and media – and they become indistinguishable and equally undesirable. An economic migrant is a threat; so is a refugee, by extension. It is acceptable racism, as long as the race is everyone outside the UK. Confuse the asylum-seeker too, with complicated legislation and procedural requirements that would stump an English-born college student: distraught and vulnerable asylum-seekers, as well as the bogus ones, are required to fill in a nineteen-page Statement of Evidence Form. This must be completed in English, and all accompanying documentation must be in English, whether the applicant speaks it or not. It must be returned to the Home Office within ten working days. In 2000 some 24,290 claims were thrown out because of a failure to conform to procedural requirements. Being dispersed from London to Middlesbrough, or not having an interpreter, are not accepted as reasons for failing to comply. It's filtering by forms, and it's unfair.

The title of the government's 1998 White Paper on Immigration was 'Fairer, Faster and Firmer'. By 2003 those concerns about firmness and fairness had changed. The new White Paper's title – 'Safe Borders, Secure Haven' – lays out the government's priorities: our borders are under siege from economic migrants, and we can only offer a safe haven once the borders are secure. In his preface, Home Secretary David Blunkett wrote that 'there is nothing more controversial, and yet more natural, than men and women from across the world seeking a better life for themselves and their families'. He meant economic migrants, not refugees. He wrote about 'those who wish to work and to contribute to the UK' before he chose to mention 'those who seek to escape from persecution'.

By 2004 the distinction had become so confused that even a supposed liberal – David Goodhart, editor of *Prospect* magazine – could write in the *Guardian*: 'Immigration and asylum: 9 per cent of British residents are now from ethnic minorities.' Fellow *Guardian* writer Gary Younge responded two days later: 'Given that more than half of non-white people were born in Britain, what does this fact have to do with immigration or asylum?'

Confusion is helped by dubious statistics. Much of the asylum debate is a game of numbers. It's rarely about people. Migration Watch, an anti-immigration group run by Professor Andrew Green, is a favourite source for statistics and comment by certain newspapers. In a letter on its website, Professor Green makes a point that he often makes. 'The real issue is not the principle of protecting refugees but the scale of abuse that has developed in recent years as the number of asylum-seekers has nearly trebled since the mid-1990s to about 100,000 a year. On average, only 10 per cent qualify under the 1951 convention but 90 per cent stay, two thirds of them illegally.'

This is true – 10 per cent of asylum-seekers do qualify under the 1951 Convention – but it's also untrue. The Convention is rarely used to grant asylum or refugee status. In total, including appeals, over 50 per cent of asylum-seekers are granted leave to remain or refugee status. There is actually no such thing as a bogus asylum-seeker. According to the 1951 Refugee Convention, to which the UK is a signatory, everyone has the right to claim asylum, and until they are refused, they cannot be called bogus. The extent to which this is ignored can be guessed by the fact that the Press Complaints Commission – hardly a biased pro-refugee organization – was moved in 2003 to advise journalists and editors that the term 'illegal asylum-seeker' was distorted, inaccurate and wrong. 'Legally there is no such thing,' it said, and mildly advised editors to be careful.

Refugee organizations blame the hostility on 'a culture of disbelief'. Unlike British citizens, who are entitled to be innocent until proven guilty, asylum-seekers are disbelieved until they can prove otherwise. They are assumed to be economic migrants – and therefore liars – until they can prove they are not. This is obvious in the language of the Immigration and Nationality Directorate, which carries out asylum interviews; official communications from this body are overwhelmingly likely to use the words 'alleged' and 'you claim to have been . . .' to the point where they drip with contempt. As the British NGO Asylum Aid points out in its 1999 report on Home Office decision-making, what's wrong with 'you said'? It goes on: 'For instance, the murder of a Kenyan woman's sister is "regrettable"; the ("alleged") death of a Nigerian's father is "an unfortunate occurrence". "Your alleged ill-treatment" is the closest the Home Office gets to acknowledging treatment that is, by all normal standards, torture.'

In response to a Cypriot man who had requested asylum in Britain because he'd been beaten and burned with a metal bar by the authorities in Northern Cyprus, the Secretary of State decided that 'taking into account your appalling lack of credibility . . . these wounds were inflicted at your own request to strengthen your claim.' The Medical Foundation for the Care of Victims of Torture, a fine and unhysterical organization, reported that a Turkish man had over a hundred scars on his back, including bruising that indicated he had been held down. An Iranian man is sent a refusal letter that accuses him of coming only for economic motives, because he is a single young man with few qualifications. In fact, his family were wealthy, but the interviewing officer had never asked that. A Colombian who reported three attempts to kill him was asked to produce his friend's death certificate. An Amnesty International report in 2004 extracted a refusal letter to a Congolese man from Kisangani, which stated that, 'The fact that fighting was taking place in this area is irrelevant, the Secretary of State can reasonably expected [*sic*] you to go to Kisangani.'

There are hundreds of other examples, none of which conform to the best practice described in the UNHCR *Handbook on Procedures and Criteria for Determining Refugee Status*: 'Since the examiner's conclusion on the facts of the case and his personal impression of the applicant will lead to a decision that affects human lives, he must apply the criteria in a spirit of justice and understanding and his judgement should not, of course, be influenced by the personal consideration that the applicant may be an "undeserving case".' If this were true, there wouldn't be one in five cases overturned on appeal. That's 15,000 cases in the last year.

There are undeniably traffickers and abusers, and those who take advantage. Writing in the *Observer* in 2003, former immigration officer Tony Saint described how Lithuanians and Brazilians would suddenly claim asylum if they were refused entry under normal visas. He writes of his time at the Eurostar terminal that, 'We had Roma stowaways under the train, Malaysians jumping off the platforms, Albanians running down the tracks to Vauxhall bringing all Network South East services to a halt.' He writes about the 'small armies of Chinese males who regularly managed to get over the Channel on the rail service that ran direct from Disneyland Paris, all dressed up to blend in'. Each of them carried a piece of paper with the name of a solicitor. 'There it was, the Geneva Convention being invoked by a group of blokes all holding silver balloons and wearing Donald Duck caps. Looking back on my decade-long career in the Immigration Service, that image just about sums it up.'

But behind the balloons and the traffickers are refugees who are falling through the cracks. The government has changed the asylum legislation three times since 1997. In their aim to 'securitize migration', they've now made it almost impossible for a refugee to enter the UK legally. They've also made entering the UK illegally a crime of detention. By the end of 2001 there were 2,800 detention places for asylum-seekers in the UK. In the 2003 White Paper the Home Secretary pledged to raise this to 4,000, because 'detention has a key role to play in the removal of failed asylum-seekers and other immigration offenders.' The primary focus of detention will be 'its use in support of our detention policy'. Fair enough, in theory. Not fair in practice: the majority of detainees are thought to be still waiting their initial decision. In essence they are criminals because they have asked for asylum.

Who are these criminals? Families, sometimes. Mothers separated from their children. They have had no trial, have no access to bail and no idea how long their sentence is. The majority of cases, according to the Refugee Council, aren't awaiting removal: they haven't even been given an initial decision on their case. They are in detention because they are flight risks. After all, they know about running. In fact, detention is about deterrence, same as everything else.

Mohamed Sonie is a single young man from Monrovia. As such, he fits the 'one-dimensional image' of a bogus asylum-seeker, as described in Article 19's report 'What's the Story?' The stereotype of the bogus asylum-seeker is young, male, swarthy, wearing a cheap leather jacket and loitering somewhere he shouldn't. He is usually to be found at the entrance to a tunnel, near a fence, or in the pages of tabloid newspapers.

Mohamed is twenty-four years old, which makes him young. He's single, because he left his family behind in Monrovia, and he has no idea if his father and sisters survived when their house was burned down in Claratown. He's even got a leather jacket. And according to NASS (National Asylum Support Services), he's bogus, too.

Being a single young man makes him a target both there and here. He is threatened at home, because all young men were targets for forcible conscription. He is threatened here, because he is perceived to be a threat.

We meet in a living room in Northampton, along with John Nimly Brownell and Daniel Draper. Brownell is chairperson of the local Liberian association, L.I.B.E.R.I.A.N., and Daniel is on the committee. This association's name is either the product of too many refugees with too much time on their hands or too many Liberians used to too many acronyms. It probably took weeks of decision-making to come up with Liberians in Britain Encouraging Reconciliation Internationally and Nationally.

L.I.B.E.R.I.A.N. has its own website, complete with ambitions – to send containers full of supplies back home – and grisly photographs. It has about fifty members in the area. The national Liberian association only has about 300, so that's good going. There is some debate about how many Liberians are now living in the UK, but it's not many. Some say 3,000, some say 5,000. Liberians say 3,000 are real Liberians, and another 2,000 are Ghanaians and Nigerians pretending to be Liberians. This certainly happens. 'Someone told me about a Liberian man who was in my hostel,' says Mohamed. 'I was really surprised, because I thought I was the only one there. So I went to see him and he told me he was Nigerian!' Mohamed shakes his head in disbelief. 'And then he asked me to help him in his asylum interviews! I said I'm sorry, man, but you'll have to use the Internet. I can't help him. He's making fun of what I've gone through. It's dirty.'

According to the Home Office, Mohamed has gone through

nothing. We meet in John Brownell's living room, because this is where Mohamed came after he was denied NASS benefits. In 2002 the Nationality and Immigration Act was passed. It changed existing asylum legislation by removing the right to work of people waiting for decisions, and a later addition – Section 55 – changed it further. To discourage fake asylum claims, an applicant could be refused any financial or accommodation support from the state while waiting for a decision on his case. In a recent report the Mayor for London's office summed up this policy as 'destitution by design'. It calculated that 200 people a week in London alone would be made destitute by Section 55 refusals. Half of these people are women. A news report in February 2004 showed a young female refugee sleeping in a telephone box. In his response to a questionnaire by the InterAgency Partnership (IAP), a consortium of refugee organizations, on the effects of Section 55, a seventeen-year-old Liberian man described how he was sleeping rough in the Underground and eating from rubbish bins. Under the heading 'feelings about experiences', the interviewer has recorded that 'he thinks he will die if the situation stays the same (broke down and wept).' Another Liberian who had been denied support was more cool-headed. 'I don't understand the workings of Section 55. I think there's a hidden agenda. It's a way of telling people not to come to the UK.' This sums up most of the current asylum policy. Deterrence, not welcome.

Mohamed was luckier. He exemplifies the IND's second-best-case Section 55 scenario (the first is if he hadn't tried to come at all): if the government withdraws support, then refugee communities – because they are warm-hearted and not politicians – will take up the burden of care. 'I was in emergency accommodation in Kent, but then I had to leave. Someone in Monrovia told me Daniel was living here, and we'd worked together in the YMCA. So I came here. Sometimes I wonder what I'd have done, if I hadn't.' There about twenty Liberians in Northampton in Mohamed's position. A penniless, boring position. Seven months on from his interview – when most asylum claims are resolved in a month or so – Mohamed has heard nothing. If the claim hasn't been resolved after six months, he's supposed to get a work permit. He hasn't got one. He hasn't got money. All he's got are empty days, some pocket change, and generous friends. 'Liberians won't see their brother down the drain and not help him,' says Brownell. 'We can't take all of them on, but we will help who we can.' Mohamed gets passed round, from spare room to sofa, to anyone who can take him in. A friend in America sends him nice clothes. Someone's lent him money for sparkling stud earrings, and now he daren't send a picture home to his mum. 'She'll think I look gay!' But no one can provide him with anything to do. 'During the week I browse the Internet. I'll go to Daniel's work and get some money, buy food and prepare it. I only really come alive on the weekends, when people are around and we can hang out.'

Mohamed's story was dismissed, to his face, as 'not credible', by the NASS interviewer. 'She was really horrible. She told my lawyer to move away from me, in case he coached me. I'd never met him before! And anyway, he was Nigerian. What did he know about Liberia?'

Probably more than the interviewer. Asylum caseworkers are supposed to rely on the Home Office's Country Information Guidelines. These provide a basic history (the history section consists of two paragraphs) and background information on the country of origin of the person they are interviewing. There are occasional bulletins, too, with copious references to situation and human rights reports, as well as newspaper articles and agency reports. But the basic reference points are simplistic: the flag (they are referred to the Flags of the World website at www.cruflags.com, which doesn't work), national anthem ('from Internet site Anthems Directory', no address given), and the *Lonely Planet Guide to West Africa*, 4th Edition, April 1999. An IND caseworker told Amnesty UK this year that 'caseworkers were discouraged from searching for alternative sources on the Internet.' Even if they wanted to.

Mohamed, Daniel and John laugh. It would be funny, if it wasn't so flawed. 'She asked me to recite the national anthem,' says Mohamed, still disbelieving that something so easy to check, in the days of the Internet, could be used to decide whether he was telling the truth. She also asked him to sketch the flag, to describe Liberian money (he took some out of his pocket and showed her), and to name the river that lies between the US embassy and the Executive Mansion in Monrovia. 'I looked at the lady and said, . . . "There isn't a river. They are all along the Atlantic coast." She said, OK. I think it was a trick question.'

Asylum Aid's report criticizes trick questions as 'crude'. In asylum interviews Kosovar Albanians have been asked to name the biggest park in Pristina. There is no park in Pristina, which wouldn't be difficult for a non-Kosovar to find out. Trick questions are easy enough; but the caseworkers aren't trained well enough to distinguish the Kosovar Albanian dialect from Albanian Albanian, thus admitting countless asylum-seekers from a poor but peaceful country (Albania) as well as those under true threat (Kosovars in the late 1990s). A Liberian accent is unique enough to be a distinguishing feature too: Ghanaians don't sound like they stepped off a Carolina plantation. Daniel Draper, like Mohamed, had been told there was a fellow Liberian in the same hostel as him. When he went to meet him, the man said his name was 'Kofi'. 'Everyone knows that Kofi is a Ghanaian name!' says Daniel in a bewildered tone. Not everyone, but a caseworker should.

Asylum specialists would like to have an Independent Documentation Centre set up. They'd also like to reform the asylum system, but not the way the government would. Before the new Asylum and Immigration Bill (first proposed in November 2003), asylum-seekers had the right to two levels of appeal. They also had the right to a judicial review, because that's been the law since 1771, reinforced in a ruling by Lord Scarman in 1974, which decided that 'there is no distinction between British nationals and others. He who is subject to English law is entitled to its protection.'

That was until Clause 10. The proposed 'ouster' clause in the new bill removes all right to judicial review or appeal to a higher court. It forbids any judicial scrutiny of deportation orders. The government calls this an improvement, because it will cut down months waiting for appeals. I call it sweeping and sinister. No fewer than sixteen members of the Matrix law chambers (though not Cherie Booth) signed a motion calling the clause 'the most draconian ouster clause in parliamentary practice'. The constitutional expert Professor Vernon Bogdanor described it as 'a constitutional outrage, and almost unprecedented in peacetime'.

In fact the clogging of the asylum system has been overwhelmingly proved to be the initial interview. Ill-prepared caseworkers make ill-advised questions and have ill-formed conclusions, which are then often overturned on appeal. Sometimes they don't get round to making a decision in the first place. Mohamed is still waiting after seven months, with no money and no work permit. 'My solicitor thinks the caseworker might have gone on holiday.' For seven months? 'Yes. Or maybe it's maternity leave.' Yes. Or maybe it's a streak of incompetence that runs through the asylum system like gold through rock, and it's equally hard to shift. 'What I knew about asylum,' a thirty-two-year-old Liberian man told the IAP questionnaire, 'was that authorities would look into your case with an awareness of international events, and give support until you're able to earn a living.' He was disappointed.

Mohamed was given a copy of the interview notes, and he gets it out from time to time, maybe to remind himself that he officially exists in some mothballed file somewhere. He shows them to me, outside the small terraced house that he's sharing with a generous South African friend – 'African solidarity' says Brownell. The questions are simple, but Mohamed's story is both simple and complicated. The simplicity first: he is a young man, and therefore conscriptable by anybody. 'They'd do random conscription raids. I had to hide many times, sometimes in the ceiling.' The complication: 'People think Mohamed is a Mandingo name. And my last name – Sonie – is used by Krahn women.'

I'm lost, and ask for an ethnic tutorial. 'LURD, the leading rebel group – the leader and most of the fighters are Mandingo. I lived in Claratown, which was government territory. Once you're thought to be Mandingo and you're living in the territory of your government, you're treated with suspicion. As for my surname, because it's Krahn, they'll consider me to be from MODEL.'

So you're damned on both sides?

He grins. 'Basically.'

John Brownell feels the need to explain further. He went to Monrovia in 2000. 'You have to understand that while the rebels held the interior, there was relative peace and civility in Monrovia. But once the rebels came, there were rumours that they had infiltrated the citizens and were only there waiting, so once a security man comes and asks you for your name – that has been the precedent in all the wars – you understand that there's no security any more. Since 1990 there have been extrajudicial killings, all kinds of horrible things happening in the city. And they just keep on repeating, 1990, 1992, 1994, 1996, 1997. You see those things occurring, you're not going to hang around for 2003! You're going to get out, right?'

Mohamed got out with bribes and persistence. The Nigerian government was providing a free plane to get its citizens to safety in Ghana, with some places for Liberians. 'You had to go every morning and bribe and beg. I spent US$40 on the bribe, but the ticket was free.' The Nigerian plane flew to Ghana. Mohamed spent five days in Buduburam camp, because that's where Liberians go – if you want to get a bus there from Accra, ask for the one heading to Liberia – before flying to Heathrow. This makes him typically African (91 per cent arrive by plane), as does his use of an agent (69.4 per cent of refugees rely on them). He landed at night, and knew enough about the procedures of asylum to ask some policemen where he should claim it. The immigration officials had long gone home, and the policemen told him to go to the IND office in Croydon in the morning. He did as they said. This delay, according to the NASS interview, meant that he had not asked for asylum 'as soon as reasonably practicable', according to Section 55. 'She asked me why I hadn't taken the badge numbers of the policemen, and why I hadn't got a written report from them!' As another Liberian refugee pointed out, 'It's not as if there's a big sign saying ASYLUM at the airport. Section 55 is not reasonable.'

Another case, where an Afghan man had been arrested by police, given a map to get to Croydon, and shown the map to his interviewer, got the Home Office response that 'the Immigration and Nationality Directorate is aware that the Surrey police do not hand out maps. IND believe that the applicant was trying to mislead.' A NASS employee I know – who was supposed to have signed the Official Secrets Act, but his employers hadn't got round to it – told me about a letter that has been sent to applicants which says, 'If you have not received this letter, please contact NASS immediately.' His job was to 'weed out people who are not eligible for benefits or who are defrauding the system. I am required to deal with people who have been tortured or abused, who have escaped from oppressive regimes, experienced brutality, survived social implosions and often been the victims of armed conflict. For this sensitive and difficult work, I received precisely one week of training.'

When Section 55 was announced, its intentions were clear. The denial of assistance was supposed to weed out those who applied for asylum once they'd got into the UK ('in-country'), limiting it to those who applied on entry ('port'). In December 2003 the Home Secretary made this clearer: if someone applied within three days, this would be understood as 'as soon as reasonably practicable'. By in-country, the government meant people who waited several days, weeks, or months before applying. They were obviously fraudulent: genuine refugees will obviously apply as soon as they land.

This is rubbish. The government's own statistics say so. Asylum applicants who had been granted humanitarian protection (i.e., the ones judged not to be lying) overwhelmingly applied in-country (87.5 per cent). If this is the basis of criteria for distinguishing economic migrants from refugees, then it couldn't be more wrong, and that's only the beginning.

In their Cricklewood living room, Grace Quoi's husband Obe keeps butting into the conversation. I'd been invited to the Quoi house to talk about Kouka Tou Non, a Liberian women's association of which Grace is president. It's interesting, if typically bureaucratic – I have to make two trips to get permission to speak to them, and explain myself thoroughly in front of a dozen sceptical Liberian women, before they decide to form a special subcommittee to explain themselves to me.

The subcommittee turns out to be Grace, her husband Obe and son Rich.

Obe fits a classic Liberian profile in the UK: 'If Liberians came here, it would only be to study, then we'd go back. I bet before 1989 you wouldn't even find a hundred Liberians living here.' This isn't ingratitude. Obe waves his hand around at their Sony TV and decent house, and says, 'I am grateful for this. I am grateful I've been here all this time, but it was never my intention.' In 1989 he was doing a postgraduate degree at a Scottish university. Five months later the war started. He didn't see Grace and his sons for two years. 'I just stayed sitting here. It was so depressing. There was no way of contacting her.' Finally they found each other in Côte d'Ivoire, and he brought the family over. Now they're all British citizens, Rich is properly British, though he's also Liberian. Obe says he's still learning how to be British. In classic Liberian understatement, it's not easy.

'I felt alien. Back home we value education a lot; it's a big thing. To come here and know you are educated and you can't find a job — it's very shocking.' He applied for dozens of jobs in Scotland and didn't get anywhere, so they moved to London. Now Obe works as a security guard for a Canary Wharf bank; he could do better, if he was given the chance. Grace is a care worker, though she's a banker by profession. They support two sons over here and dozens of people in Liberia: Grace has twenty-two brothers and sisters. 'People don't understand what it's like,' says Obe. 'They say, "Take tomorrow off," and I say "No! I can't afford to," and I beg them to let me work.'

There are other things people don't understand, or choose not to. Little things, that you don't see until it happens to you. Kouka Tou Non was set up as a 'social safety net', because there was no other provided. Grace is a friendly, warm woman, but after ten years here she had so few friends, she decided to recruit some. It started when someone died. 'You British, you just sit alone in a house with your grief. We can't do that! The Jewish do shivas, and we call it "sitting on a mat". We will come to your house for a week straight and sit on your mat, and share your grief.' That became Kouka Tou Non – 'we are one' in Kpelle, the language of Liberia's biggest ethnic group. 'We are refugees. Even if we have status to live here, we've still got a stigma, so we help each other.'

Obe decides to put on a video. It's *America's Stepchild*, a 2002 documentary by Liberian film-maker Nancee Oku-Bright. Grace's son Rich was nine when they left. I expect him to be uninterested: he's a young man, and his girlfriend is round for a visit, and there must be other things he wants to do more than getting roped in to sitting through the Liberian equivalent of a Christmas home movie. But he's engrossed. Dead bodies lie in the street, and he says. 'I remember that! That's what the streets looked like.' Intellectuals are interviewed – ex-president Amos Sawyer, Archbishop Michael Francis – and Rich says, 'Congo [Americo-Liberian] people talk differently, don't they?' They would, says Obe, who is not Congo. 'When your first and only language is English, you speak it better.'

The video provokes lively discussion. They must have seen it dozens of times, but it still causes arguments. A political dissident appears on screen and Grace tuts. 'The country wasn't ready for dissidents!' Obe is impatient. 'Don't be ridiculous – we had 122 years of independence. How much readier do you want a country to be?'

They go on to talk about the Americans. Obe is scornful. He takes the cynic's role in the household. 'Americans save us? No way. No way! In Sierra Leone, Britain felt it had an obligation to save them. But the Americans felt nothing.'

Why would they, someone sniffs. The rubber was all gone.

★

In the Article 19 survey, only 13 per cent of newspaper articles gave any sense of the reasons refugees leave their country. In the White Paper, David Blunkett didn't seem too interested in their reasons, either: 'The Government and those agencies and organizations delivering nationality, immigration and asylum services need to demonstrate that they know what they are doing, and that they do it well. Only in this way will we be able to expose the nonsense of the claim that people coming through the Channel Tunnel, or crossing in container lorries, constitutes an invasion when it patently demonstrates how difficult people are finding it to reach this country.' Not that it demonstrates that fearful people will take desperate measures to get to safety.

Still, in the same White Paper the Home Office set out its desire to institute a resettlement programme. This is an unequivocally good thing. Other countries have these – the US lets in over 70,000 refugees a year – but the UK has never had a proper scheme. There has been the oddly named Ten Or More resettlement programme for disabled refugees organized by UNHCR (it does what it says: countries take ten or more disabled refugees and their families). There is a 'mandate scheme' administered by the British Red Cross, under which a UNHCR-identified refugee at risk in their current country of asylum may apply to resettle in a third country. There have been the occasional mass country evacuations, for Bosnians and Kosovars. And now there is a new, apparently permanent programme for the resettlement of 500 refugees worldwide into the UK. It all sounds great, according to Home Office correspondence: 'This offers a legal route for genuinely deserving cases [that] will help to ensure that we are offering protection to those who need it. The vast majority of refugees are unable to pay traffickers and remain in their area of origin often in very difficult circumstances.'

The 500 quota for 2004 is supposed to be made up of Liberians. The screening was supposed to take place in Ghana, by officials flown there specially, and the first batch of sixty lucky Liberians was scheduled to arrive in late January. But they didn't. Nor did they arrive in February. The Home Office could offer no explanation why. I asked them to tell me more and they declined. Refugee organizations also refused to comment on the programme, while the Home Office only said this: the resettlement was part of a 'balanced immigration strategy – tackling abuse of the asylum system by people not in need of protection, open managed migration routes and better integration of those with the right to settle here'.

I read this with irritation. Press office nonsense. But actually it said more than I'd thought. Not just in the logic of its sentences – the priorities plain as ever – but in the manner of its obfuscation. It sounded like fear. Officials were terrified of the media finding out about the resettlement programme, because of a climate that official government policy has helped to create. Yet compared to the US resettlement programme, the UK's is spindly. It works out at 0.008 per cent of the population, compared to America's more generous 0.02 per cent. The US has more land, for sure (29 people per square kilometre, compared to our 244), and ours is a small and crowded island. But still, when even little Denmark can take twice as many resettled refugees as us, with a tenth of our population, I smell official cowardice.

There is fear, also, in the relative deluge of legislation being put out. A massive Nationality and Immigration Act in 2002 was followed by a new Asylum and Immigration Bill only a year later. 'The frequency of legislation itself,' wrote the Refugee Council, '[creates] the impression that the system is not working.' The new bill will abolish the two-tier system of appeals; currently 41 per cent of asylum-seekers get decisions overturned on appeal. The new bill exudes mean spirit and massaged asylum figures. When it was announced in early 2004 that asylum applications were down by 40 per cent (to 61,050), the government was gleeful. Refugee workers weren't. That would be fine, they said, if the world had got 40 per cent safer.

But the state of the world can seem an afterthought, when it comes to asylum policy. According to the Foreign Office travel advisories, I am advised against all travel to Liberia. The country is too dangerous for me, and all travel insurance is void. But it's not too dangerous to send failed asylum applicants back there. In 1997 only 14 per cent of Algerians were granted asylum in the UK. In 1998 this number leapt to 88 per cent. Nothing much had changed in that time: Algerians were still getting their throats cut by government forces and Islamist rebels. No reason was given for the change in policy. There is sometimes no logic to the policy itself: in 2002 the Foreign Office was asking for sanctions on Zimbabwe for human rights abuses, while the Immigration department refused to accept that Zimbabweans had any reasons for leaving their country.

On occasion the reasoning is explicit. In late February 2004 the prime minister had talks with Tanzania. The UK government offered to pay the Tanzanians £4 million in aid. In return Tanzania would take all the UK's failed Somali asylum-seekers and stick them in a camp. The government calls this a Zone of Protection. Critics call it passing the buck: responsibility is shifted to poor countries who do most of the job of housing refugees already. Camps are never a good idea. Refugee-bargaining is nothing new – the UNHCR is constantly begging countries to take refugees, presumably with some carrots – but for a government to admit it so openly was something different. Given the public hostility to asylum-seekers, to sell them off is politically acceptable. (Tanzania apparently declined.)

★

None of the Liberian refugees I meet complain about their situation. It's better than being dead or injured back home. But if they have the chance of being not dead and not injured but back home, I think they will take it. A Sudanese woman, in the Article 19 survey on media stereotyping, said, 'I have got my own position in the central bank of Sudan. My husband used to be the governor of a state there, so coming to their country is not a privilege to us. It is just to protect ourselves from different things . . .'

Anti-immigration lobbies think asylum-seekers have ideas above their station. In fact, they're all working far below it. 'I don't want to criticize what I've got,' says John Nimly Brownell, in his comfortable sitting room in his comfortable semi-detached house. 'But people don't realize – in normal conditions I'd be in a much better situation if I lived in Liberia.' John is a physicist. He used to be a teaching assistant at the University of Monrovia, and now he sells furniture. 'I don't know if it's because of racism or what, but I had fifty interviews when I came here. And every single one, the same thing: "We wish you luck in your endeavour, but . . ." I'm wasted here. Wasted!'

Daniel Draper has Extended Leave to Remain until 2006. This is actually out-of-date; ELR is now known as Humanitarian Protection, and is given to people believed by the IND not to be proper refugees, but whose country is undoubtedly in a mess. Daniel used to work in the YMCA in Monrovia. He says wistfully, 'I had twelve people under me. I had four people who had to report to me weekly.' He went to the YMCA in Northampton to ask for work, but they wanted a British qualification in social work, and Liberians follow the American education system. Also, they said, young kids wouldn't understand his accent. He's not offended by this, though I think it's insulting, as his English is certainly understandable. He's just annoyed they wouldn't let him work for them. He's also insulted by his workmates. 'They say to me, "Why are you sending money home? Is that the only reason you're here? It is, isn't it? You're just here to earn money and send it out of the country."'

Daniel shakes his head. 'I say, "But what's wrong with that? I pay taxes. I have people who are living off what I earn."' So he's at fault if he earns money, and he'd be at fault if he were on benefits. Scrounger or exploiter, in the eyes of the British public it's the same difference.

In Sheffield Alfred Nagbe's living room is a feast of technology. His television set is man-size. His computer is new. His mobile phone is a few generations ahead of mine. Alfred is thirty-four and supports twenty-two people. He sends home as much as he can a month, usually about £200.

Alfred was my pet project. I'd asked in Monrovia and Côte d'Ivoire for people who had relatives in the UK. But nobody did. They were all in New Jersey or California. Who'd want to go to the UK? Finally, on the way to Nero Village, the IRC staffer Simon-Pierre remembered that he knew someone who might fit. We stopped at a house, and children poured out of it, followed by a large woman in T-shirt and lappa, and a thin man. The woman was Viviane Toh, the man was her man, and none of the children belonged to her. They'd all lost their families, and she'd taken them all in. While Viviane told me her story with typical Liberian haste and practicality – 'I was attacked five years ago and I was raped and I'm still in pain' – her man ran into the house and brought out a piece of paper with Viviane's brother Alfred's name and address on it. I copied it down. But none of it worked, when I tried it. My pet project didn't have prospects.

After a week a thought occurred: maybe a refugee wouldn't

scorn phone books like the British do. No one I know is in the phone book, because not being in it is thought to be safer. But if you're from Liberia, where landlines died out in 2002, and phone books are a hilarious concept, perhaps a phone book represents safety. Perhaps it means you do exist, somewhere. You are less invisible. This may be fanciful rubbish – but he is listed in the phone book.

Alfred answers the phone, and doesn't sound particularly surprised to hear about his sister, though he hasn't seen her for two years. He says it's fine to visit, and will I be staying the night? What would I like to eat? Should he come and meet me at the station?

I'm expecting a family man. He's expecting a Liberian. From the pause of surprise after he's looked through his spy-hole, I can tell, he is trying to figure out what a white woman is doing at his door. My name could be Liberian – I met more Georges in Liberia than anywhere else, ever – and my interest in him must be Liberian too. It can't be British.

He gets over his surprise, and I get over mine, because he's alone. But then I have another surprise, when I ask how he got here. 'I came to be a priest.' He did priestly studies with the Carmelite order in Liberia, then in Ghana. They paid for his school fees in his home town of Greenville, where he grew up and stayed put, despite its being bombed by ECOMOG fighters trying to flush out Charles Taylor. The first time ECO-MOG came, it was almost amusing. 'They came to disarm Taylor. But he disarmed them, took their cars and sent them back to Monrovia.' The second time, they didn't bother with the cars, but sent the 'du-du boys' instead. The what? 'The jet fighters. I don't know why, but we called them du-du boys. They'd bomb in the day, and the gunboats would launch rockets at night. They were launching at Taylor, but they didn't know where he was, so as soon as they saw a group of people they'd bomb them in the hope of hitting some rebels. They had a 75-calibre gun on the planes. And the shells – if one of those touches you, it's very terrible.'

As usual, there's always worse. That was in 1992. In 1993 the Liberia Peace Council rebels came with warlike intentions. 'I was at home when they came. They asked everybody to leave the town so they could come in and loot.' They found one Krahn man and 'they did what they call *tabbé*: they tie his hands really tightly behind his back, so the skin goes through the flesh.' Then they cut his throat and drank the blood, while everyone was watching. 'They believe it gives them power, it makes them more evil. It gives them some evil from the dead man.'

After that, Alfred waited for things to calm down. He was going to be a priest, and had faith in fate. God proved him right, when the rebels kept coming to his school to recruit all the pupils, and the Carmelite sisters kept going to negotiate with the general and succeeding in diverting his attention from the school pickings. But when NPFL came back in 1994, the sisters were told the situation was too dangerous, and they had to leave town. Alfred left too, aiming for Côte d'Ivoire. His mother didn't want to travel. 'She said she was used to the town, and rebels didn't bother with old women. Young men – they either make you fight or they think you're a rebel. If they meet you, they'll usually kill you.' Even so, he set off with his cousin, a pair of nice white and black Converse sneakers on his feet, fresh from the States and a generous Carmelite contact. He didn't have them long, not surprisingly: he was close to not having his life for long either. 'They pointed their gun and told me to take my shoes off. I wanted my life, so I did. I remember it was the WILD unit of NPFL. They were very fierce. They had girlfriends who stood behind them telling them what to take.'

He had money too, for a while. 'We walked for a week, eight hours a day. I was carrying $1,000 Liberian [about £10], but I hid the money in my briefs and I think one of the rebels saw it bulging and he took it.' Then they told him to carry a gun. 'One of those you mount on a pickup. There was a creek and there was a heavy flood and they couldn't cross. So they took the gun off the pickup and were looking for people to carry it on their heads. They got ten of us to carry it. They were shooting between our legs, saying they didn't want LPC to come and take the gun, so to hurry up.' His cousin managed to make herself a nuisance by crying, so they let Alfred go. 'I'm glad – they wanted us to carry it a very long distance: [as far as] from here to Sheffield town centre.' Since we're in an outlying council estate off the Chesterfield bypass, I ask for clarification. It was ten miles.

He reached Gozon, where I met his sister Viviane. She was still stuck in Liberia at the time, working in a gold-mining town in Sinoe county. Alfred was taken in by a Krahn man, but he didn't feel safe. 'There were no Ivorian soldiers patrolling, so Taylor soldiers could come all the way to Gozon like it's Liberia.' He stayed there for a couple of years, then went to Ghana to go to school. Ghana is English-speaking; Côte d'Ivoire isn't. He headed for Buduburam and rented a room with a Liberian woman in the camp.

'I was supposed to do my priesthood training in Zimbabwe, so in 1998 I went to Monrovia to get a passport. It was supposed to cost US$20 but actually it was $150. You have to bribe, obviously.' He stayed in Ghana but kept visiting Monrovia, then applied for a study visa for the UK. Denied. 'They thought I didn't really want to study. So I went to university for a year and studied philosophy and reapplied.' Granted.

The Carmelites paid for his ticket and housed him in East Finchley. The studies were at the International Missionary

School, where there were two other Liberians, Eric and Joe. 'I came in September 2002 and in January they asked me to leave.' I look at him closely. His manner is unemotional, usually, but here there's some irritation. 'They said they thought God wasn't calling me to be a priest. I thought he was, but they disagreed.' And – according to Alfred – all Christian hospitality was stopped. They offered to take him back to Monrovia, but only a fool would return in early 2003, when rebels held half the country and the *Economist* decided it had the worst prospects in the world. Alfred became an asylum-seeker, and now he wants to become a refugee. There is some irony here: you live in a camp in Côte d'Ivoire and you're stigmatized as a refugee. Fly to London, and being a refugee becomes something to aspire to.

He went to the immigration office in Croydon, and asked for refugee status. 'They knew my case, and they knew the situation in Liberia. They were nice to me.' Still, his application for refugee status was refused. He was given Exceptional Leave to Remain, and the chance to reapply in 2004. He fetches his documents to show me. He keeps them under his mattress, despite a surfeit of storage space in his flat. His accommodation wasn't always this nice. 'They put me in a hostel in Lewisham. It was all single men, from Guinea, Sierra Leone, Asia. After two weeks they sent me a letter saying I had to come to Sheffield. I had to go and look it up on the map.' Straight up the M1, and into the unknown. 'I was a bit worried, because people in the hostel would say that places outside London are more racist, because they aren't used to foreigners.' The racism wasn't the problem, though. 'They put me in Park Hill, but I didn't like the environment. There were too many drugs. It wasn't clean.' There wasn't much room for improvement, beyond some furniture he was given by the charity St Wilfred's. 'I had vouchers that they took in Sainsbury's, Somerfield. It was £30 for two weeks.'

How on earth did you live on that?' 'I managed. You have to.'

The scrounging refugee signed on at the Job Centre as soon as he could, and got a temporary job at Cadbury's. He was good at it, and got a staff job, to run a machine that wraps sweets. Now he earns £14,000 a year, pays taxes, does what he's supposed to do. Life is OK. Not like last year, when the World Wars were happening, and he felt like he was stuck in treacle. 'I couldn't help them! I'd phone up, and you could hear the guns launching down the phone. I couldn't even send money because they'd closed Western Union because soldiers used to go and harass people collecting money. Then my niece's phone went dead. I was calling and calling, and it was always the same – "The LoneStar phone you are calling is either switched off or out of coverage area." . . . "The LoneStar phone you are calling is either switched off or out of coverage area." . . . "The LoneStar phone you are calling is either switched off or out of coverage area."'

Alfred thought this meant death. His family was behind LURD lines, which became government lines, which became LURD lines again. For a while he followed events on the news, but it was too hard. 'It lasted two weeks. I couldn't watch TV, I couldn't read the papers. All I did was go to work, come home and try to phone and go to sleep. Sometimes I'd go to sleep at 2 p.m. and wake up the next morning.' Eventually, the niece answered. Her battery had gone dead. There was no rice to eat in Monrovia by now, let alone mobile phone batteries.

How do you recognize a refugee? By the size of their phone bill. Alfred's is large, but he can afford it, because he does nothing else. 'I don't go to pubs or anything.' Not even with your workmates? 'They've never asked me.' He goes to work, watches the Original Black Entertainment channels, phones Monrovia and sleeps. That's it. Don't you even rent out videos? 'No. They have African films on OBE. That's all I'm interested in.' Behind closed doors, he lives in a little piece of Liberia. It's a comfort.

I give him a lift into Sheffield. He's taking driving lessons – with the AA, 'because you have to have standards' – but for now takes the bus everywhere. He chose this flat because it's on the number 53 bus route, a direct line between his council estate and Cadbury's, every ten minutes. He got the flat in an auction. He knows more about bureaucracy than I do. 'I've signed more forms in this country than ever in my life. Why do you need so many forms?' I drop him off in the Saturday afternoon crowds. It's a cold, foul day and I thought he had an errand to run. 'No. I'm just going for a walk.' And he walks off, alone, looking cold in his winter coat. I watch him in the rear mirror, and think of the photograph he's got on his mantelpiece. It's of a chubby, grinning man I don't recognize. 'That's me!' says Alfred, who is skinny. 'That was me in Ghana last year.' When he came to England he weighed 80 kg. Now he weighs 65. If asylum is a numbers game, then 15 kg in a couple of months is as good a number as any.

Alfred is, by all terms of reference, a successfully integrated, productive refugee. He is part of the invisible presence in the asylum debate, which is fixated on threatening, abusive, illegal young males. As such, he would never feature in the pages of our newspapers, and he would never want to. This is typical, as is his hard-working, low-profile behaviour, according to the Article 19 report. 'Not least of the findings reported here is the reluctance of newly arrived asylum-seekers and refugees to challenge the way they find themselves misrepresented in the press and broadcast news. Characteristically, they want to keep a low profile, they don't want to make a fuss, they simply want to get on with their new lives and not draw too much attention to themselves. It sounds very much like living in fear.' It also means they're the perfect victims: pick on asylum-seekers and refugees, and they'll rarely answer back. They are the trash can for all politically motivated xenophobia. This is why the leader of the British National Party has said that the asylum issue legitimizes his party. Every bigoted headline recruits another new member.

In Monrovia, Gayah and I are sitting in Sam's Barbecue. He's asked the waitress the vital question: 'Do you have any food?' Now, as we wait for spice and rice – this is a country where the 'bitter ball' vegetable is considered a delicacy, whereas I consider it to be a lethal weapon – we are talking refugees. Gayah is only the second person I've met during this trip who has never been displaced. The first was Vera, whose family was killed by ECOMOG rockets, and whose apartment building sheltered 4,000 people during the World Wars. She had sixteen people in her two-room place. 'They wanted to sleep in the bathroom too, but I wouldn't have that.'

So Gayah has never been a refugee, and he doesn't intend to be one, if he can help it. A year ago he was sent to the UK for a two-week training course. 'The first day I went to the tube station. It was Goodge Street. I saw this man cleaning, and I thought, he really looks like an old friend of mine. But I didn't disturb him, because I thought it couldn't be true. Next minute, he's looked up and rushes across to hug me. The first person I see in the UK and he's a Liberian!'

The tube cleaner's name is Jude. When Gayah knew him, he was at medical school and Gayah was at university. 'In 1991 he was given the opportunity to go to the UK and he did, and now he's been sweeping for ten years. He can't come back home because he's doing two or three jobs and he's still got nothing to show for it. I gave him my address in London but he never found time to meet me. I don't know why. Maybe he was too proud. Maybe he was ashamed of me seeing him like that.'

I ask Gayah if he's envious of refugees who get to the UK. He shakes his head, over a Club beer at a table across the road from Samuel Stryker's funeral parlour, in a city where death is still very close. He says no. 'Because they have secondary school education or something but they will end up working as subway cleaners. They have no idea.'

They have even less idea, now, under a legislative onslaught that even I find confusing, and I'm supposed to speak the language. What chance has a refugee got? 'You've hit the nail on the head,' says someone in the Refugee Council's press office, who has spent ten minutes patiently explaining clauses and sections and the nuts and bolts of a mean and shameful asylum policy. 'These are very worrying times for refugees. Very worrying.'

In 2002 the Home Office commissioned research into why asylum-seekers choose to come to the UK. They found several reasons: because family members were here; because it's an English-speaking country; because it is perceived to be a tolerant and democratic place. In this tolerant and democratic place, people cross the road when they see Mohamed Sonie. Sometimes they spit, too. He thought that was a cultural quirk that he wasn't aware of, until someone told him otherwise. 'When I was at the accommodation hostel in Kent,' he says, in a calm voice, 'we used to play football every night. Every night, local kids would fill up bags of stones, go up to their flats and throw them at us. The police would come, stay for a while and leave, and then they'd start throwing stones at us again.' He looks at me, shakes his head, smiles at the thought. 'Crazy.'

'I heard through the media that the UK is a first-class place for human rights,' a now-destitute Liberian told the IAP questionnaire. 'But it's not so in practice. I came to the UK because I thought asylum meant seeking refuge to protect your life. But the process is degrading. I'm sleeping in the streets around Manor House [north London]. I can't get support, I've got no housing, I can't work, I can't go to school. How is a man supposed to live in a situation like that?'

# 11. Totalpeace

*On UNMIL radio:*
PRESENTER: What would you say to the UN?
GIRL: I would say, 'Thanks!'

It's party time at Monrovia's Mamba Point Hotel. A Belgian airline is hosting an event to celebrate its new routes into Liberia. All of Liberia's finest are here – the foreign minister, also known as the leader of MODEL – the deputy Libyan ambassador, who stayed in his embassy during the World Wars One, Two and Three, because he had to. 'The Sierra Leoneans abandoned their embassy, and it got looted.' There are businessmen and women. The room smells of power. Even the US ambassador is here, with flashing lights and armed bodyguards. He is a good man, they say, and embarrassed about his country's failure to intervene militarily in Liberia. The British honorary consul is here too, as he invited me. He's jovial, mildly mocking. 'You want to write a book of Liberian horror stories?' he says. 'That would be too easy.'

There is bad red wine and fresh Club beer. Too fresh, I joke to the Swiss director of the Club Brewery – I've heard complaints about insect remains and the high levels of formaldehyde used to keep the insects out. He's very offended, and lectures me on brewery hygiene. Fair enough, but Club hangovers are fierce and stabbing, and they feel more toxic than usual. The British honorary consul will only drink Heineken.

The Club Brewery lies in LURD territory now, on Bushrod

Island beyond the port. It's not far from the carwash where an IRC vehicle was commandeered by a LURD general, because he felt like it. The vehicle was returned, but then the company responsible for cleaning it sent it back to the same carwash, where a LURD member was hanging around, because there are LURD members hanging around all over Bushrod Island. The LURD man said, 'But that's the general's car!' and it was gone again. So it goes.

At the party there is an air of self-congratulation, thanks to the Belgian airline. The new routes are money for them, and a sign of business confidence for Liberians. It is one of the few signs of confidence here. Mostly, Monrovia is prey to hope and exhortation, not conviction. It's a city of pleas. Posters, signs, shops: 'Drive carefully!', 'Treat a person with AIDS as your brother!', 'Don't pass on second-hand smoke!', 'Liberians must rid themselves of the vices which cause war!' There was one sign that was particularly memorable, painted on a piece of board stuck in the ground alongside Tubman Boulevard: 'Time is running out for Liberia.' It has an exclamation mark, too.

In the spacious office of Monrovia's Archbishop, there is none of the air of congratulation of Mamba Point. Michael Francis is a fearsome figure, in the best way. For years he criticized Charles Taylor in public, which counts as reckless bravery here. In 1996 Taylor's NPFL forces put a gun to his head when they decided to ransack his house. 'I said, "Go ahead, kill me now! I'm not afraid of you." And the man backed off. He was afraid I was going to punch him in the head.' Archbishop Francis is an impressive man, and Liberia needs more men like him. An Irish missionary priest, not given to hyperbole, says, 'He's the kind of person who is needed to hold together any kind of hope at all.'

Liberia is being held together by hope and by UNMIL.

Neither should inspire blind faith. On 7 December 2003 UNMIL decided to hold the first round of disarmament, in Camp Schiefflin north of Monrovia. A nice ceremony was organized and all went according to plan. Women in cocktail dresses, nice speeches. Then the dignitaries left, including UNMIL's general, Daniel Opande, and most of the security forces. The NGOs and few UNMIL staff who stayed on faced 8,000 former fighters who had turned up at the camp to relinquish their weapons in exchange for cash. This round of disarmament was supposed to be for former government fighters only, but rebels from LURD and MODEL had arrived too. They all wanted the cash, and they wanted it immediately. (Some of the government fighters hadn't been paid for two years.) They had their weapons, or some of them, and they were prepared to hand them in for the US$75 they'd heard would be paid on the spot. Except that wasn't UNMIL's original plan: the 'reinsertion allowance' was supposed to be paid only after ex-combatants had gone through three weeks of reintegration, and the rest – of a total of $300 – after further stages of the reintegration process. The fighters had other ideas. They wanted the $75 immediately, but there was no money on hand and not much security. There were 8,000 grumbling armed men and women. It was a powderkeg, and it blew.

'It was a mess!' says Allen Lincoln of Don Bosco homes, whose staff were there to help run the reintregation programme. 'They said they were expecting 1,000 people and 8,000 turned up! They weren't even ready for 1,000. There was no food. There were no mats to sleep on. There were no buckets to take baths.' Worse than that, the UNMIL staff who were supposed to conduct the initial interviews – What's your name? Who's your commander? Where did you fight? – didn't understand Liberian English, and some weren't much better at any other type of English either.

Lincoln gets irate when he thinks about it. He has good reason: the next day, the fighters went back to doing what they do best. They jumped in their pickups and went rioting. The result was three days of looting and violence that left seven people dead. A peacekeeper from Benin was shot in the leg. The city was terrified, and the damage was deep: Liberians watched as UNMIL stood back and didn't intervene for three days. A western diplomat says that's normal. 'They do that all the time. I saw a man stripped naked and beaten in front of a Pakistani peacekeeper. He was just sitting on his tank, watching.' Allen Lincoln raps the table with fury. 'I tell you one thing. God help us. If those three forces [ex-government fighters, plus rebels from LURD and MODEL] had just had the thought to say, let's get together and take on UNMIL, Monrovia would have been in hell.' An exasperated UNMIL official told the International Crisis Group that 'we can only expect better things in the future or it will be war.'

The best solution for a refugee is the most durable one. The most durable solution is for a refugee to go home. The most durable home is one that is safe. Everyone agrees on those points. No one agrees on how to reach them. On 18 February 1943 Joseph Goebbels asked a rally at the Berlin Sportpalast, 'Do you want total war?' The crowd yelled, 'Yes!' When you ask Liberians what they need to be able to go home, they are equally adamant. Totalpeace. One word. Totalpeace is the durable kind, not what they've seen before, throughout the dozen ceasefires and fifteen sets of peace talks since 1989.

'I don't feel 100 per cent safe,' says Naomi Lewis, the nineteen-year-old leader of the girls' group at Maimu IDP camp in Liberia. 'I feel 75 per cent safe, and for the other 25 per cent we need Totalpeace.'

Within Totalpeace, everyone has their own shopping list.

'I'll go home when I don't hear guns any more,' says a woman in Totota IDP camp. 'I'll go home when UNMIL deploys in Lofa county,' says another. Or 'when there is deployment and disarmament,' say illiterate peasant women in English, using perfect peacekeeping terminology. John Nimly Brownell, from his Northampton living room, says he'll go home when they've had elections, scheduled for 2005. But what about your English wife? 'Oh, she knows I'm going back. I love Liberia. I'm going back.'

Some are already marching homewards. Literally. A news agency reported in January 2004 that 10,000 people had moved back to Liberia from Sierra Leone between October and December 2003. Some went on 'go-see' visits – go over, report back. But most set off home, walking doggedly. UNHCR had nothing to do with it. The refugees had decided there was enough peace to try.

But is there? The transitional government is stuffed with military men. The peace talks in Ghana were such a greedy scrabble for the best state jobs, the process began to look like legalized looting. The chairman of the government, a neutral businessman called Gyude Bryant, is paralysed between the factions. 'Civilians have no role in this government,' a LURD official told ICG. 'They are virtually voiceless.'

This isn't hopeful. Nor is the presence of Charles Taylor in Nigeria. He's left the stage, but being in Nigeria counts as being in the wings. Nor is the statement by Chairman Bryant that a truth and reconciliation commission will rock the peace process. 'There is absolute impunity and arrogance,' says Archbishop Francis. 'There are criminals in government who were there when Samuel Doe was in power! These things have a way of coming round in a vicious circle. We need a war crimes tribunal and a reconciliation commission. Everything.' A country that has suffered civil war has a 46 per cent chance of lapsing back into conflict within five years. Liberians probably know that already.

Some ingredients are already in place for Totalpeace. There's the biggest force of peacekeepers in the world, if it ever gets to full deployment (at the last count, it was 6,000 men short). There is Jacques Paul Klein, the UN Secretary-General's Special Representative to Liberia, a forceful American who is not afraid of whipping things into a shape he likes the look of: he said in January 2004 that soldiers were only good 'for playing cards and plotting coups', which is impressive when the government is full of them. There is some money available. At the UN donor conference in early February, donors pledged US$520 million for Liberia's reconstruction. It was a big deal, symbolized by the fact that the meeting was co-chaired by UN Secretary-General Kofi Annan and US Secretary of State Colin Powell. The UN had requested $488 million, but the donor countries decided to be generous. At the end the total was read out, as if it was reconstruction bingo. Everybody clapped. Everybody was satisfied they were doing a good thing.

This is true. But they could do more. The money is going to reconstruction, not to emergency assistance. A country on its back needs a little help to stand up, let alone walk around. The donors virtually ignored the separate request for $137 million for immediate assistance. UNICEF needs $6 million to provide education to Liberia's children, but it's been given only half. The UN asked for $50 million to fund DDRR (disarmament, demobilization, reintegration and rehabilitation), but it has received only $9 million in pledges. The US occupation of Iraq, by way of comparison, costs $3.9 billion a month. This is the 'burn rate', according to Secretary of Defense Donald Rumsfeld, in his testimony to the US Senate. If Iraq's burn rate was cooled down for just a few days, Liberia would have all the money it needed.

That's not a throwaway comment. We should pay attention to little Liberia. It's insurance. In its 2003 report 'Breaking the Conflict Trap', the World Bank – not renowned for its left-wing policies – found itself with liberal sympathies, because they coincided with being financially conservative. The global incidence of civil war is high, it said, because the international community has done little to avert it. 'Inertia is rooted in two beliefs: that we can safely "let them fight it out among themselves," and that "nothing can be done" because civil war is driven by ancestral ethnic and religious hatreds.' It's short-sighted and dangerous.

The World Bank highlights three rings of suffering caused by civil wars. First, displaced people strain the resources of neighbouring countries. Secondly, civil wars produce territory outside the control of normal governments where drugs and weapons can flourish, all the way to the western world – for example, 95 per cent of hard drug production comes from countries with ongoing civil wars. And thirdly, not dealing with civil wars costs more in the long run: 'Several civil wars reached a point where intervention became unavoidable. Bosnia, Cambodia, El Salvador, Haiti and Rwanda and Somalia cost $85 billion.'

A Home Office study by the refugee policy expert Roger Zetter said it plainly enough: refugees are forced to flee their homelands because of conflict and persecution. Refugees are 'policy resistant'. All the claims that asylum-seekers are mostly economic migrants are demolished by statistics; the top refugee-producing countries are systematically the ones with problems. In the last six months of 2002, the top three, with 35 per cent of the total, were Iraq, Zimbabwe and Somalia. Refugees will try to come, no matter how high the wall or how harsh the policy, because they have to. They will only stop coming when there is no reason to come any more.

'Governments,' wrote Professor Zetter, 'should direct their attention to these root causes of displacement' – rather than build bigger walls. Bigger walls cost more money, for a start. The legal and other costs of an asylum-seeker in Europe are US$10,000, said David Blunkett in 2003. By contrast, he said, the UNHCR gets by on US$50 a head. Making it impossible to enter the country legally encourages traffickers and agents. It criminalizes refugees by default, because they have no choice. Making everyone illegal makes it harder to track them, so a competent asylum policy – one that is 'fairer, faster and firmer', for example – becomes impossible to run.

Legal, working asylum-seekers awaiting their case decisions might displease the Home Office, but they could please other government departments such as the Department for International Development. Alfred Nagbe, sending his £200 a month back to Monrovia, and all the other Alfred Nagbes who send money home each month, bring developing countries more money than government aid, private bank lending and IMF/World Bank assistance, according to World Bank figures from 2002. They would please the Treasury too: a Home Office study in 2001 calculated that migrants – including refugees and asylum-seekers – pay 10 per cent more into the Treasury than they take out.

UNHCR figures count 20 million people worldwide as refugees, or 'persons of concern' as they put it. A *Times* poll in 2003 found that 34 per cent of the British public thought that asylum was the most important issue facing Britain today. If only they meant that they wanted to solve this issue, not push it away.

There are plenty of 'what ifs'. What if US troops had gone ashore in full force into Monrovia in 1989, and stopped fourteen years of war with a little extra effort? What if someone had noticed that Côte d'Ivoire is paying US$600 a head in its disarmament programme and that Liberia is paying $300, encouraging the movement of armed boys, girls, men and women? What if immigration caseworkers changed their benchmarks, so that they started from the supposition that not everyone is a liar, and that refugees are survivors – of rebels and soldiers and war, of international inaction, of anything the tabloid media can hurl at them – not victims? What if they bothered finding out that Kofi is a Ghanaian name, and Mohamed can be a Liberian one? What if the media heeded the advice of the Press Complaints Commission and learned that there's no such thing as an illegal asylum-seeker? What if the constant use of 'illegal asylum-seeker' counted as a hate crime, because that's what it is?

Refugees don't bother with such speculation, though. What's the point? Proper speculation is better spent on deciding whether it's better to have all four limbs amputated in Sierra Leone or be killed in Liberia (the correct answer, according to one refugee: be killed in Liberia). Proper speculation is waiting to see if you can stand still after fourteen years of running, if you can plant your rice, keep your clothes on, get a work permit. As for the rest, say with a smile, like a Liberian, but from the heart, 'It's not easy. Ha!'

# *Acknowledgements*

Thank you most of all to every Liberian and Ivorian who shared their story with me in Monrovia, Totota, Salala, Kakata, Tabou, Nero Village, Abidjan, London, Sheffield and Northampton. Thank you for your frankness and humour, and I wish you everything you wish for – home and shelter, Totalpeace and no more bulgur wheat.

Thank you to everyone at the International Rescue Committee, including Nicky Smith and staff in Monrovia, Julien Schopp and colleagues in Abidjan, and Jennifer Walsh and everyone in Tabou. IRC UK were invaluable facilitators, as was Robert Warwick, IRC West Africa Regional Director. Thanks to Julie Coski for a fine lunch on a tiring day, and to Amadou Koné for his dreadful Nagasaki song.

Thank you to every NGO worker, diplomat, academic, politician and indiscreet chatterer in West Africa, and a few outside it. Thank you to the makers of Club beer and Flag, and to the Liberian and Lebanese staff at the Royal Hotel, especially for the post-interview drinks and the demonstration of na-foot.

Thank you to the Women's Health and Development Programme for permission to publish their short stories for the first time. Thank you to the Mennonite Central Committee and Canadian Foodgrains Bank for 'In Exile . . . for a while'.

Thank you to my readers and calmers-down Tom Ridgway, Sheila and John Wainwright and Lisa Margonelli, who were always on hand to alleviate doubt, bad temper and panic.

Thank you, lastly and notably, to Mary Mount at Penguin

Books for having had the faith to commission me to write this book, and for her skills in encouragement, editing and Liberian map-reading.